HERITAGE OF LAKELAND

'How fortunate those who live within the shadow of the fells. What a heritage to guard and to share.'

A. Harry Griffin

HERITAGE
OF LAKELAND

A CENTENARY COLLECTION

A. HARRY GRIFFIN

EDITED BY PETER HARDY

F

FRANCES LINCOLN LIMITED
PUBLISHERS

Frances Lincoln Limited
4 Torriano Mews
Torriano Avenue
London NW5 2RZ
www.franceslincoln.com

Printed and bound in China

1 2 3 4 5 6 7 8 9

CONTENTS

Part Three
Fell and Rock Climbing Club – *Journal* articles

Part Four
Mountains and Music

Part Five
A Lakeland Year – *The Guardian,*
Country Diary pieces, 1951 to 1979

LIST OF ILLUSTRATIONS

1. A. Harry Griffin, the young Coniston Tiger
2. Harry and Mollie
3. Coniston Tigers Hut
4. Harry Griffin, *Daily Mail* journalist
5. Harry Griffin. Army portrait
6. Harry Griffin at Imphal
7. Harry and brother Les
8. Harry at the Matterhorn
9. Harry's father, Arthur Griffin
10. Harry climbing on Shepherd's Crag, Borrowdale
11. Sandra, Mollie and Robin
12. Harry skiing on Raise
13. RSPCA award presentation
14. Harry and Mollie opening of The Griffin Bar
15. Sambo, a faithful companion
16. Sgurr Alasdair, Skye
17. Harry sailing off Vancouver, Canada, 1984
18. Wedding day 1989
19. Harry, 91 years of age
20. Coniston Tigers Log Book
21. Coniston Tigers Log Book
22. Walking Diary

All images courtesy of Sandra Parr

INTRODUCTION

This book has been compiled to mark Arthur Harry Griffin's centenary year. Born on 15 January 1911, Harry died in 2004 aged 93, after a writing and journalism career spanning more than seventy years, during which he documented and reflected on every aspect of the Lake District – from the fells and crags, the flora and wildlife, the ancient history of Roman forts and mysterious stone-circles, to the rich heritage of folk and farming traditions. He also vividly describes Lake District personalities and characters from shepherds to hoteliers, pioneer rock climbers to eccentric hermits.

Harry climbed and walked in north Wales, Scotland, the Alps and Canada and a small number of pieces have been included to reflect his travels and holidays with family and friends.

The selection of pieces includes some of Harry's contributions to *Cumbria* magazine, *Lancashire Evening Post*, *The Guardian* (Country Diary), the *Journal* of the Fell and Rock Climbing Club and passages from his final and unfinished manuscript Mountains and Music. Also included are the complete contents of a slim, handwritten Coniston Tigers Log Book that was discovered in Harry's papers after he died. Believed to have been written by Harry in 1932, these notes provide a brief glimpse at the early days of the Coniston Tigers, their rock climbing expeditions and life at the famous climbing hut. A number of walking route outlines from Harry's personal notebooks have been selected for additional interest. These source documents are held in archive by the Fell and Rock Climbing Club.

Readers may note that in some passages Dow Crag is referred to as 'Doe' as this was still the commonly used name for the fell in the 1930s, when Harry was climbing the soaring rock of Dow, or Doe, with his fellow Coniston Tigers and members of the Fell and Rock Climbing Club.

The rest I leave for Harry Griffin to say in his own masterly words.

ACKNOWLEDGEMENTS

Sincerest thanks to Sandra Parr, Harry Griffin's daughter, who has collaborated with me for a second time to produce this book. It has been a great pleasure to have the opportunity to read through her father's personal papers in order to research the pieces and notes that have been compiled and I am privileged to have been given the opportunity to work with the writings of A. Harry Griffin.

Thanks also to John Nicoll and his talented staff at Frances Lincoln Ltd.

Thanks are expressed to the Fell and Rock Climbing Club, in particular Peter Smith, Archivist for the Club, and to the staff at Cumbria Record Office – Kendal, especially Richard Hall who assisted with research of Harry Griffin's personal scrapbooks (Ref: WDX:1488).

Thanks also to Peter Richardson, Features Editor at the *Lancashire Evening Post*; Paul Jackson – Editorial Director and Kev Hopkinson – Features Editor both at *Cumbria* magazine, Martin Wainwright – Northern Editor of *The Guardian* for contributing his Appreciation and Bill Birkett for providing the captivating image on the jacket cover.

Finally, thanks to my lovely wife Jayne.

Peter Hardy

HARRY GRIFFIN – AN APPRECIATION

Harry Griffin was a champion of the north. His beat was the Lake District, especially above the 1,000 feet contour, but his values were those of the region more widely. His writings reflect the sturdy independence, perseverance and love of wild, open spaces typical of those lucky enough to live between the river Trent, comfy Cheshire and Hadrian's Wall. He was an explorer too, another characteristic of Northerners who have something of Captain Cook, child of Teesside and Whitby, in the way they deal with the world.

Harry travelled overseas, serving in military intelligence in India and skiing in Canada, but he made his most precious discoveries in the hills above his home. He knew the Lake District's fells backwards, up-and-down, disguised by snow and shrouded in mist. He tucked himself into the tiny rock cabin near the summit of Bowfell, which he rediscovered and nominated as England's highest 'house.' He reunited lost walkers before marching on. He found exciting deviations off the tramline guidebook paths and gave hints, but no more than that, for enterprising readers to sort out routes themselves. He was born and bred in these parts. For all his military bearing and bristling moustache, which could have earned him the retired general's part on any village hall stage without make-up, he was a lad from Barrow-in-Furness who understood how the world worked. His first outing to the rock faces was with George Basterfield, Mayor of Barrow and a man absorbed in making a success of a major industrial town. This was far from the idyll of shepherds and poets which form an imaginary Arcadian Cumbria in outsiders' minds.

Harry saw and described the hard work behind the beauty of the hills and lakes. He knew about the quarrymen, for example, and in great detail. Not just the slate mines of Honister or the rock hacked away around Castle Crag, which have been much-described. But such fascinating specialities as the diatomite found in the Kentmere valley, highly-valued for its use in polish and drinks filters. He was an expert as well on the wall-builders, the Manchester waterworks engineers and the shivering, soaked farmers hunting for cragfast sheep. The latter impinged on his own life, often. His medals drawer included several certificates for helping rescue the daft animals from their fixes, with slings, ropes and the occasional, encouraging kick up the backside. He was a do-er, you see, another northern characteristic and one which gives further strength and distinctiveness to his writing. Like all of us who enjoy the Lakes, Harry took much from the mountains, from the first day that he set out with the lads who were to become his fellow 'Coniston Tigers' in endless assaults on Dow Crag. But he gave, too. He was prepared to sit for hours on committees, to argue the dull details over access, or the path of pylons, and to encourage the young, through spare-time work for the Scouts and climbing organisations.

Let us remember as well that he was a journalist, and a fine one. He ran the Lake District coverage of the *Lancashire Evening Post* for decades, and his 53 years of writing *Guardian* country diaries provided a small but important portal to those who decide Britain's national affairs. He was both a scoop man, famously in the case of Donald Campbell's Bluebird tragedy, and also buccaneeringly inventive. When the BBC asked him too late for an eyewitness account of floods in Kendal, he put a muffled microphone out of his office window and recorded evening rush-hour traffic. It sounded sufficiently like the Kent in spate. That deadline-beating side to his life shows in the simple clarity of Harry's work.

There is little here of the writing for effect which smells of the lamp and seldom outlasts its own time. Instead you will read straightforward accounts of life and journeys in the nearest that this blessed plot has to Heaven. And you will get to know a good companion as you march along.

Martin Wainwright

PART ONE

Lancashire Evening Post – Leaves from a Lakeland Notebook articles

THE TURKEY RUSTLERS
20 December 1946

Lakeland's 'little season' begins this weekend, and will last for one week – in some cases, a fortnight. Most of the hotels – even the recently de-requisitioned ones – will have plenty of visitors and, from what I can gather, there will be no noticeable lack of Christmas fare. One hotel manager who is expecting more than one hundred guests told me there will be turkey for everybody, although I do not expect all the hotels will be quite so fortunate.

The police, by the way, are still keeping a close watch on the few turkey farms in the district, and so far I do not think there have been any coups by the turkey rustlers we hear so much about. One police report I was shown said the footprints around an unlocked cabin in Westmorland had been found, upon examination, to be those of policemen! So that's fair enough…

But having finished with the 'little season' the Lake District has perhaps only four months in which to prepare for the American tourist 'invasion' which really means so much to our prosperity. It is easy to foresee difficulties here, but it is reassuring to learn that the Government's new central tourist board, the Travel Association and our own Morecambe Bay and Lake District Resorts Federation are already getting down to the problems. We want the Americans – bluntly, we need their dollars – and we also want our own people from the towns and cities.

Now that most people are getting holidays with pay, and there is talk of petrol going off the ration soon, we can confidently expect 1947 to be a bumper year for British visitors alone. Obviously many of the present difficulties now handicapping any attempts to increase the accommodation potential of the district – shortage of labour, shortage of materials, and food and fuel restrictions – must be eased considerably. This must be done, too, without any detriment to the pressing housing problems of the district, and the ever present need to preserve the amenities. Here's a big job for a big man who can work fast.

I am writing these notes after three successive nights of frost in Lakeland and, like many scores of others, I am keeping my fingers crossed for a chance of some ice skating this Christmas time. My last venture was, I think, in February, when I performed alone on virgin ice on Goat's Water under Dow Crag near Coniston. Strange how the quality of ice varies in Lakeland. On this occasion the ice was principally frozen sleet and you could drive your heel into the water beneath quite easily, and yet not crack the ice. At other times I can remember black ice on Styhead Tarn and white ice on Sprinkling Tarn only a mile away but 500 feet higher.

My memories of skating in Lakeland are not very old, but I can recollect skating on Windermere about twenty years ago, when there were scores of motor cars and braziers on the ice. We don't seem to get frosts like that now.

One of my favourite skating grounds has always been Tarn Hows, 600 feet up and normally one of the earliest places to freeze. My happiest memories are of Tarn Hows in the moonlight, with the dark woods framing the prettiest picture.

It is strange how the real experts you meet on the ice are nearly always fairly elderly people, despite the pre-war growth of skating palaces in the cities. I suppose one reason is that many years ago one could always count on something like a month's skating every winter, whereas nowadays one is lucky to get a weekend.

CONISTON UNDER SIEGE
13 June 1947

There have been hundreds of people visiting Coniston for the first time in their lives this week who seem to have been quite content to wander with the crowds down the old road trying to catch a glimpse of Sir Malcolm and his Bluebird, without a glance at what has always been Coniston's principal attraction – the Old Man. Despite the ugly scars left by the quarrymen, Coniston Old Man remains one of the best loved of our Lakeland tops, for in many ways he is an extraordinary mountain. His summit is the highest point in Lancashire; he presides over his own very distinctive group of fells; the best slate in the world is quarried from his slopes; he is flanked by one of the most magnificent crags in Britain; he is jewelled with four lovely mountain tarns and he has even been climbed by a man on a motor cycle.

But perhaps the most extraordinary thing about the Old Man is his name. Why is he called the Old Man? Well, I've heard a lot of learned explanations from time to time including all sorts of Norse derivations but I think the answer is probably the simplest one of all. Most of the names of our Lakeland fells have simple local origins and I do not think it is necessary to talk about the Norse words 'alt maen' – I forget what they mean – or make any other wild guesses. I am pretty sure that the 'man' simply refers to the cairn on the summit, which, in the years when the name was coined, might have been in some way remarkable. The present cairn, built, I believe, by the Ordnance Survey, is a massive affair – although I have known it completely hidden under 12 feet of snow – but Coniston folk have told me that in former days there used to be three cairns on the summit – the old man, his wife and his son.

For the second time in eight years, Coniston finds itself in the news and besieged by crowds of men and women of the press, films and broadcasting. Naturally the village has taken kindly to them, for being in the spotlight brings business. Ever since 1860, when the branch railway was first run in from Foxfield for the copper mining industry, Coniston has endeavoured to attract the people.

There is no mining in the Coppermines Valley now, but

the village is as thickly sprinkled with hotels and boarding houses as any other tourist centre in Lakeland, and new private hotels spring up every year. But, like business folk anywhere else, these Coniston people have been finding it difficult, or even impossible, to get new telephones installed so that when they heard that two extra telephones were being installed especially for the Bluebird adventure, some of them grumbled. "We've been waiting twelve months for a telephone, and still no sign," they say, "whereas these people come along for a fortnight and get everything fixed up right away."

In point of fact, the first arrangements about the extra phones were made some time ago and I can speak from personal experience about the apparent inadequacy of the normal Coniston telephone facilities when coping with an emergency. I believe there are normally only three lines out of the village – an extra two were being added this week – so you can imagine the chaos when perhaps forty or fifty newspaper men want to contact their offices at approximately the same time. Quite apart from the present abnormal demand on the Coniston telephones it would appear that if only three people in the village were ringing up say Kendal, Ambleside and Windermere, there would be no line available for an accident or fire call.

At the time of writing these notes I do not know whether the two extra lines will be permanent, but I am sure the Coniston folk could think up some sound arguments for their retention.

HOUND TRAILING
29 August 1947

More people are nowadays watching hound trailing in Cumberland and Westmorland than ever before – the bigger fixtures attract football match crowds – and I feel that before next season some major reorganisation of the sport is desirable. In my opinion, it is in the quality of the sport as a spectacle where there is most need for improvement. I do not believe – as I have been told – that people only go to hound trails to back, or try to back, winners. Most of them also go to watch the trails and, in too many cases, they are not getting their money's worth.

Too often we see the hounds released, disappear over a shoulder of fell half a minute later, and then – nothing for perhaps twenty minutes or more. At the end of that time we might catch a glimpse for a minute or so of some undistinguished specks coming down from a distant slope, and then, perhaps nothing more until the leading hounds come into view a few hundred yards away. This does not happen every time, but happens far too often. Hound trailing, the summer sport of tens of thousands, with its setting among the finest country in England, should be a spectacle and, as such, the trails should be visible over as much of their length as possible.

As everybody knows, these 'unseen' trails are liable to arouse suspicion, and one still hears of allegations of unsavoury work going on behind walls, in woods and on remote slopes far from the field. I would like to see a big effort made next season to keep the hounds in view for as long as possible. New centres should be chosen, trailers should be paid more money for laying the trails, and finishes visible for only perhaps a quarter of a mile should be banned. I know the HTA has made some big improvements already, but they are still – in my opinion – not giving enough for the spectator and there should be much more imagination shown in the laying of some of the trails.

Every effort, too, should be made to guard against these void trails. In some cases, I have been told, the mixture may have been at fault, but this does not explain everything. In this hot weather some of the trails are much too long.

SNOWDONIA
3 June 1949

It was almost with a feeling of relief that I drove north into Westmorland the other day, and saw the familiar shape of the Lakeland hills in their purple evening gowns, after a non-stop run from Wales. For a week I had been living beside the placid waters of Llyn Ogwen, in Snowdonia, and, much as I admire this rugged mountain country, I always experience there a sense of desolation and even oppression which I have never felt in the Lakeland hills. It is really remarkable that the characteristic mood of the two most comparable mountain districts in Britain should be so violently opposed – one of them smiling, friendly, compact, and so full of exciting variety and colour, and the other, wild, a little forbidding, sombre in its grey, treeless slopes, and in places, almost awe inspiring.

A Welsh farmer, living simply without even the sparse comforts of many Lakeland farmers, confessed that even he found his mountains "a little sad." He was not thinking of the many mountain tragedies there in recent years, but was peering back down the centuries into the agonies, sorrows and mysteries of his race.

The first thing the Lakelander would miss in the mountains of North Wales would be the trees, which give his native land so much of its colour, and the next thing might be the camaraderie of the fells and dales. We were on the crags and ridges every day and never saw another soul, and you might travel the valleys all day and never get to know a Welshman. And the mountains. Lakeland has no mountain to compare in form with Tryfan, no high level walk to compare with the Snowdon Horseshoe, and no crag to compare with Clogwyn Du'r-Arddu. Tryfan, a true rock mountain only has equals among some of the peaks of Skye, and is as dear to the men of North Wales as Great Gable is to the Lakelander.

I have two wonderful memories of Tryfan. One is of a winter's day many years ago when, standing on the summit I was the subject of the little seen 'Brocken Spectre', and the other is of one angry day of cloud and shadow, last week near the top of the North Ridge. A great Lancaster bomber like a monster black raven crept round a shoulder of Pen-yr-Oleu-Wen, and swept roaring down the Ogwen Valley 200 feet beneath us. We felt we could have dropped a stone onto its wings.

But there is another respect in which North Wales differs greatly from the Lake District and that is in the matter of manmade desecration. No doubt there are people in the Lake District who would like to see a railway to the top of Helvellyn but, having seen the Snowdon railway on many occasions, I am not one of them. There are the littered remains of power and water schemes in many parts of the mountains and double lines of overhead telegraph lines right through the main valleys. The ugly, double lines of poles and wire running through the lovely Ogwen Valley would, I think, shock even the most redoubtable Lakeland campaigner for 'essential services before amenities', for the dales folk, living under very bad conditions, still have no electricity.

I think our campaigners might also be slightly shaken to see the squat, ugly wooden building built at the very top of the pass at the side of the lake. In position it would compare with a building by the side of Styhead Tarn, underneath Great Gable. I lived for a week in this building, now a climbing hut, but built only a few years ago, I understand, as a private house. How the plans came to be approved I cannot imagine for there were planning standards in existence even before this new Act. I should think that if a similar plan were to be submitted today to one of our Lake District planning officers, that gentleman might never recover from the shock.

Critical though I am of the situation and appearance of this hut, I must admit that its creature comforts were superior to those of any mountain hut in Lakeland. We made our own electricity for lighting, used Calor gas for cooking, had running hot or cold water at any hour of the day or night, and enjoyed the comforts of two baths, two showers and a drying room. There is a lot to be said for cooking for oneself nowadays. I went off very greedily with some of my family's rations, did a little scrounging in Wales, and cooked myself porridge, bacon, egg, sausage and tomato every morning for breakfast.

I returned to Lakeland to hear another plea for electricity supplies for our valley folk, and to hear stories of babies brought into the world by candlelight. It is wrong that only those who can afford to install electricity generating plants should be enjoying this essential modern facility in some Lakeland valleys. We were fortunate in our electricity starved Welsh valley for, as I said, we were able to make our own. I have not noticed this particular contrivance used in Lakeland, although doubtless many of our farms do use it. The wind drives a little windmill on the top of a mast and this operates a dynamo, which generates electricity. At night the windmill made a little noise, but this was the only inconvenience, and we had electric light whenever we wanted it – free.

Many Lakeland folk, particularly in the Patterdale area, will know two of the friends I left behind in North Wales – Mr and Mrs Briggs of the Pen-y-Gwryd Hotel. These charming young people were members of the Ullswater Hunt, and fished and shot around Brotherswater. They had many tales to tell of old Mr Macpherson from this valley, who taught them most of their open-air lore. The Pen-y-Gwryd Hotel is comparable to the Wastwater Hotel in Lakeland. It was the place where mountaineering and rock climbing in North Wales was born and Mr Briggs, whose visitors' book goes back to the middle of the nineteenth century, insists that the sport began here before it did at Wasdale Head. Here you may meet the modern Welsh 'tigers' of the sport and argue with them about the respective merits of Cumberland or Caernarvon rock.

In one instance, Mr Briggs perhaps has one up against the Wastwater Hotel. I do not think – although I may be wrong – that any reigning monarch has ever visited this Cumberland hotel, but a photograph in Mr Briggs' entrance shows the present King and Queen in the hotel garden apparently having afternoon tea. It was taken either during or since the last war.

DRYSTONE WALLS
24 June 1949

Perched on the summit ridges of many of our Lakeland fells – notably at the top of tracks climbing up and over the ridges to the valley below, you will find, stark and ugly against the skyline, crude iron stiles, perhaps 4 or 5 feet high standing quite alone. Of course, as the iron fences, of which they were once a part, have disappeared, they are never used, and they merely serve as rusty reminders of an age when apparently people seemed to have money to burn. For the scores of miles of iron fences crisscrossing our Lakeland fells, sometimes almost on the 3,000 foot contour, can never have been much use. They were but poor substitutes for the drystone walls, they did not keep in the sheep and as boundary indications they were almost a relic of feudalism.

I do not know of any of these high fences which are still kept in repair – the valley fences, of course, are a different matter – and I would like to see an effort made to remove the miles of straggling, purposeless, old iron and wire, which disfigure many a fellside. Might there not be a job here for the Friends of the Lake District or the other amenities societies? It would be a big job but a thousand resolute mountain lovers should be able to do a fair amount of clearing up in a year.

At the same time they might do worse than get to work to clearing away or levelling up the hundreds of rubbish heaps which pass for cairns, on many Lakeland fell trods. Cairns are all very well in their right places, but hundreds which have sprung up in recent years are completely unnecessary and undesirable. Despite the quoted remarks said to have been made by one of the Members of Parliament who came down off Scafell Pike to Esk Hause the other day, it would almost be difficult for the proverbial 'blind man on a galloping horse' to lose himself on this track, and scores of other tracks, although not so well marked as this, are quite needlessly littered with cairns – mostly in the wrong places – every few yards.

I have mentioned our drystone walls and I am often asked how old they are and how they came into being. Most of them, I have always understood, were enclosed by Act of Parliament, and it is stated that between 1760 and 1840, seven million acres of England and Wales were enclosed. One writer has stated that in 1794 it was estimated that three-quarters of Westmorland with an area of more than 400,000 acres was common land but that seven years later 10,283 acres had been enclosed. And by 1840 most of the county – and much of Cumberland as well – was within drystone walls put up with tremendous expenditure of human energy.

But many fine, old walls were built hundreds of years before then, and, for instance, the boundaries of Rydal Manor are said to have been built in the thirteenth century, and many other manors with many square miles of common land were similarly enclosed in the Middle Ages. Miles of these old walls – some of them several feet thick – have fallen into ruin, and sometimes you find just a few yards of wall high up on a fellside which seem to have been built for no apparent reason. Fell farmers, however, must keep many of these old walls in continual repair for often they are used to keep sheep away from precipitous rock faces. One such wall

– not nowadays repaired – was the Old Wall on Pillar Rock.

The other day I found another short length of drystone wall high up on Eel Crags above Newlands. It is rather sad that the old art of drystone walling is being lost. Those wallers of 100 years ago, and earlier, knew their jobs and much of their work will stand as an unchanging memorial through the ice, snow and gales of centuries to come.

LOST IN THE HILLS
2 February 1951

Searching for people lost in the Lakeland hills can be a very depressing and disappointing business but sometimes it can have its compensations and last Sunday was such an occasion. It was rather a miserable morning in Langdale. A nasty drizzle of rain had followed the brief early snowfall, a dank mist hung down low across the valley, blotting out even the nearer crags, and the only cheerful note in the gloomy outside world was struck by a group of young people tumbling about in the snow near Dungeon Ghyll on their first skiing lessons.

We were taking it easy beside a cheerful fire, secretly trying to think up excuses for not going out, but arguing that it was quite a good thing to get wet through every Sunday when we were told that four people were believed to be missing on the tops. It looked as if they had been out all night. Now this sort of thing has happened often in Lakeland, and it has so often turned out that the 'victims' were not missing at all, but had merely dropped down into another valley, that it is pointless to get all excited and start running up and down the fells with stretchers and brandy. Where, for instance, should we go? They might be anywhere. And this is the real danger of these false alarms. There may come a time so far as the dales folk are concerned, when the cry of 'wolf' has been made too often.

But, to return to my compensations, we eventually gave up thinking of more excuses for not going out, decided on the course which we thought might be wisest to adopt, and set off, with ropes and ice axes, for the gullies of Great End. Rossett Gill always seems an awful pull and it was particularly unappetising on Sunday in the rain, soft snow and thick mist, for we were hurrying. But then, just as we were kicking steps up a slope of frozen snow near the top, we saw we were climbing into what seemed an entirely new world. It was one of the finest transformation scenes I have seen in Lakeland. One moment it was wet, dark and miserable; the next, clear and distant snow-covered tops reared out of the mist like Himalayan giants, the mist and the rain swirled beneath us, and we stepped on the hard, crunchy snow of the plateau into a cheerful, white world, lit by the morning sunshine. It is moments like these which make the hills really worth while and we got on with our job with renewed strength and determination.

As it happened we found nothing, and when we got down in the evening we learned that the missing people had turned up, but we did not regard it as a wasted day. The 'lost' climbers have made a handsome apology, and do not deserve criticism except for one omission, which I must mention here, so that other people, who might be similarly placed, do not make the same mistake. Although their car, sleeping bags and other equipment were in Langdale obviously indicating they had planned to return there that night, and although they were safely down in Eskdale in the early hours of the morning, they neglected to inform the police or anybody else that they were off the mountains. Had they done so, the police and dales folk in three or four valleys would have been saved much anxiety and inconvenience. I will not labour the point more, for I know this experienced party will not offend again, and nobody could be more sorry than they are.

One further point. Is it not time that police officers

in central Lakeland who may be expected to go out on these searches were given suitable equipment for the job? The police officer who accompanied our party had no nailed boots and had to do his work hampered with a cumbersome, completely unsuitable uniform, a heavy cape, and his police cap, which he had to carry in his hand most of the time. Despite these difficulties he did exceptionally well, but he would have been most seriously handicapped if the conditions had been any worse.

I know that the county of Westmorland always seems to be financially embarrassed but surely the Standing Joint Committee could afford to spend perhaps £100 on a few pairs of properly nailed boots, some light windproof smocks, half a dozen compasses, one-inch maps, small rucksacks and so on. If, say, only one set of this equipment could be placed in each of the valleys of Langdale, Borrowdale, Wasdale and Eskdale, many conscientious police officers would be much better fitted to take part in this unenviable part of their duty. Perhaps somebody in authority might note this suggestion and act upon it.

THE MAGICAL ISLAND
25 May 1951

After walking and climbing on mountains for more than a quarter of a century, I can honestly say I have never spent a more wonderful day in the hills than I did one day last week in the magical island of Skye. It was late afternoon when we sank down on the tiny summit of Sgurr Alasdair, the highest peak in the Cuillin, after a 1,000 feet high rock climb in the sunshine up one of the vertical walls which circle romantic Coire Lagan, and prepared to take things easy for a while. For the first time, for an hour or two, we were able to study the view in comfort, and say that it was breathtaking.

From our perch about the size of a dining table, the rock

walls up which we had swarmed dipped down to the airy ridge joining the thirty or so jagged peaks of the Cuillin and all around us the mountains soared like giants' castles, the sun still clinging in places to the gullies and crags. We could see and identify every peak in the range, and indeed, we almost felt we could have tossed a stone onto the nearer ones, so brilliantly clear was the afternoon, but even this magnificence was overshadowed by the view out to sea.

As far as the eye could see the waters of the Atlantic danced and glistened, in mile after mile of Mediterranean blue and gold – everywhere 50 miles of ocean but looking only a tenth as far away were the islands of the Outer Hebrides – Harris, Lewis, North and South Uist and the rest – so clear that you could even pick out the colourings of the fields. Rum, with its fine rampart of mountains capped by its own private cloud formation, seemed almost at our feet, and, further round, the islands of Eigg, Muck, and a dozen more, looked dazzlingly clear. To the east and the southeast lay the mainland, mile after mile of scores of snow-capped peaks, and shining in the sunlight, 50 miles away across the sea and the land, towered Ben Nevis, the highest mountain in Britain. Although so far away, we could see and identify the different crags on which we had spent happy days in other years.

Not a breath of wind stirred the air and the smoke from our pipes floated straight up into the almost cloudless sky. The only sound was an occasional 'swish' as a slab of melting snow, somewhere far below us, peeled off the crags and slithered into the corrie, steaming in the heat 2,000 feet below our eyrie. The hum of insects in the bracken which one would expect on a Lake District hilltop was missing, for in Skye the top 1,000 feet of the mountains are solid rock and there is no grass, bracken or heather to be seen.

It was while we were pleasantly toasting ourselves in the sun – the weather was much hotter than you were having in the northwest of England – that we saw one of the best sights of the week. As I lay drowsing, I sensed a shadow passing the sun, and, turning my head, we both had the good fortune to see a magnificent eagle circling our summit. For two or three minutes we had him under observation, sometimes looking up at him while he slowly banked and soared, and, more often, looking down on his tremendous wing span as he dipped towards the corrie and then circled over the ridge and into the next valley. We judged his wing span to be about 7 or 8 feet and the pinions, like outstretched fingers at the ends of his powerful wings were particularly noticeable. His wings seemed very shiny and dark, nearly black, and there was a lighter coloured section along the leading edge of each wing.

We confirmed later in the evening from the farmer in the valley that it was, indeed, an eagle, although there seemed no possible doubt about it, and I have since established, to my own satisfaction, that it was, in fact, a golden eagle, despite the appearance of its colour in the air. It was the second eagle I have seen in flight in the British hills – the first one was in the Isle of Arran – and it was a sight very well worth remembering. The unhurried, apparently effortless flight of the great bird was immensely attractive to watch, and it was particularly noticeable how, on the instant, the eagle could accelerate to an exciting speed.

Well, that was our day, one of several magnificent days, but it was not over yet. As mountaineers we could not have visited Skye at a better time for, apart from the long days of unbroken sunshine, the fantastic visibility, the gay music of the burns and the warm feel of the rocks, there was always the snow. There are two ways of coming down off a mountain at the end of a hard day which bring joy to the climber's heart – a long scree run or a long snow glissade, and of the two the second is incomparably finer. This was the method we were able to use every evening in Skye, and there can be no better appetiser for dinner after a long, tiring day.

One of the finest scree runs in Britain, when it is in

good condition, is the Great Stone Shoot, dropping down from Sgurr Alisdair almost to the waters of the lechan in the corrie under the crags – something up to 2,000 feet of descent. This scree was nicely covered in snow soft enough to slide so that a standing or a sitting glissade from the top of the mountain to near the foot in a minute or two could be contrived. One moment, one could be sweltering in the sunshine more than 3,000 feet up, a minute or two later, one could be swooping downwards in an exhilarating flurry of powdery snow, and a minute or two later still – if you felt tough enough – you could be plunging into the dancing, sunlit waters of one of the finest little tarns in Scotland.

And to finish off the perfect day there was the trot down through the heather with the shadows lengthening across the hills and an evening breeze stirring the broom by the side of the burn, while one tried to guess what's for dinner, and you felt you could eat a man off his horse.

It is far from easy to compress impressions of my annual visit to Skye in the space of one column, and I realize as I finish that I have told you nothing of many wonderful days, of the lovely sea journeys, of the magic and colour of places like Mallaig and Kyleakin. These you must picture for yourself.

THE KESWICK BROTHERS
19 October 1951

An energetic eighty-year-old Keswick business man, who is still active enough to go to Switzerland every year, is now probably the last Lakeland link with the great days of sixty years ago when the new sport of rock climbing was being pioneered on his homeland crags. Until the other day there were two of them, distinguished links with happier days, but now they have laid Mr Ashley Abraham to rest in the shadow of the fells he loved so well and there is only his elder brother, Mr George Abraham, to remind us of those heroes of the end of the last century – Owen Glynne Jones, Haskett-Smith, John Wilson Robinson and the rest. Probably nobody did more for the sport than these two vigorous personalities – 'the Keswick Brothers' – as they were known even in many foreign lands, for they pioneered many of the earlier climbs, photographed them, wrote books and guides about them, and served in high office as the mountaineering clubs were formed. Their sound advice was always available, and their advice was worth taking, for, so far as I know, they never had a serious accident.

Scores of people must have first been attracted to the crags of Lakeland and later to the Alps and elsewhere by the photographs taken half a century or more ago by these young men and still on view outside the well known premises of the old family firm of photographers and publishers in Keswick. These photographs show determined looking men with large moustaches, battered hats and tremendous nailed boots in almost grotesque positions on more or less vertical pieces of rock, but no matter the situation, they appear to be perfectly composed and even happy. Sometimes they are balancing, with almost carefree abandon, along a knife-edged arête with sheer drops below them on either side; other times, tip-toeing on a single nail, they are reaching around some vertical corner overlooking space, while in many of the photographs they may be seen muffled up to the eyebrows, among vertical ice and snow, but showing no signs of alarm. These resolute men are roped together, but it looks probable in many cases that if one were to fall the other would follow him. Modern belaying methods had not been invented, and these old pioneers apparently relied on their own tremendous strength of arm and shoulder to safeguard their companions. Quite obviously the climbers of those days were men of muscle as well as courage. Most of these photographs were taken by the Abraham brothers, and in many cases it is the brothers who are in the most desperate positions on the rocks. If the climbs were possible they could do them.

The earliest record I can find of the redoubtable brothers is in 1892, when the two of them, with George the elder brother leading, made the first ascent of Walla Crag Gully, which is on the first crag on the left of the Borrowdale road after leaving Keswick. It is not a particularly inviting sort of place, but it is 165 feet long and contains three chimneys, a certain amount of vegetation and some loose rock. Although rarely visited it is still a recognized route today but the interesting point is that it was the very first climb ever to be made in Borrowdale. Now there are more than a hundred routes in the valley.

George Abraham – he had his eightieth birthday last Sunday – was then twenty-one-years-old and Ashley was sixteen. They had then been climbing for some time, but it was probably about this time that they realized the potentialities of photographing the new sport, and after this their cameras went with them on the crags. How they managed with the heavy, cumbersome cameras of those days I cannot say, but we all know that some of the results were almost miracles of artistic perfection.

After this first piece of pioneering the Keswick brothers turned their attention to the great crags of Lakeland and you will find their names in the list of first ascents on nearly all these crags. They also went further afield to North Wales, to Glencoe, to Skye and then to the Alps, pioneering and photographing all the time until to some people mountaineering and the Abrahams seemed almost synonymous terms.

The modern climber is rather apt to think rather patronisingly of the old pioneers, because of their apparent preference for wet, dark, strenuous gullies, rather than the airy walls which are more the fashion today. Nowadays, we call the period when the Abrahams were climbing the 'Gully Epoch', and look upon the old pioneers as men who were never really at home unless they were climbing through a waterfall, and digging holds out of mud with frozen fingers. But undoubtedly the Abrahams and the others who climbed with them were men of considerable resource and determination. They climbed in all weathers, they were always venturing into the unknown, they knew nothing of the safety methods practised today and, at the beginning, they climbed in ordinary heavy, hobnailed boots or, at times, in stockinged feet.

So far as I know, the two brothers only gave their names to two climbs in the Lake District – both of them on Dow Crag – but their memory will also be kept green by the well known Keswick Brothers Climb on Scafell which they made just fifty-four years ago. I believe the last climb the two brothers did together – and probably the last time either of them climbed in the Lake District – was the New West Climb on Pillar Rock, which they ascended with another old pioneer, the late Dr Collier, in 1936. The brothers made the first ascent of this exactly fifty years ago, and it is still regarded as one of the pleasantest climbs on the Rock.

Mr George Abraham has certainly some wonderful memories to look back on, and I hear that he is looking forward next year to his annual visit to Switzerland, which the brothers first visited in 1896. In that year they made one of the early ascents of the Matterhorn, and only a year or two ago Mr George went some way up the mountain during his holiday.

Scores of old climbers, many of them very well known names indeed, attended the funeral of much loved Ashley Abraham the other day, and among the mourners was the best known Lakeland hotelier of the olden days – Mr John Ritson Whiting formerly mine host of the climbers hotel, the Wastwater Hotel at Wasdale Head, who is eighty-four years of age. Mr Whiting, who remembers the Abraham brothers as lads, and has watched Lakeland climbing almost from its birth, was paying his last respects to a very old friend.

LUG MARKS
16 November 1951

Many years ago, long before the waters of the new
Haweswater first swirled over the site of the old Dun Bull
on Mardale Green, the merriment at the annual shepherds'
meet, they say, went on without a stop from the Friday
morning to the Wednesday night. Licensing hours, if there
were such things in those days, simply did not count.
Although I well remember the old Dun Bull, with its
pleasant low rooms, clean whitewashed walls and lovely
view from the porch, I never attended a shepherds' meet
there, but I do know that tomorrow's Mardale meet, held
well away from the high fells, will have little in common
with the meets of long ago.

It seems rather a pity that this year the Mardale and the
Troutbeck shepherds' meets are to be held on the same
day, the reason apparently, being that tomorrow is the most
convenient day at Troutbeck for the hounds. Mardale is
normally held on the third Saturday of the month, whereas
Troutbeck is most often a Thursday meet, generally the
Thursday after Mardale. The clash is likely to affect the
numbers of sheep at each meet for Kentmere heafed sheep,
for instance, are liable to stray into the collecting areas of
both meets, but the hunting men are looking forward to
sport at least as good as in recent years.

The Mardale shepherds' meet was held at the Dun Bull
for about 100 years, but in the very old days before that it
used to be held on the top of High Street, the 2,700 feet
high plateau-like barrier between Mardale and the Kirkstone
fells. The highlight of these old meets used to be the horse
racing held along the summit ridge, and I have seen a print of
the extraordinary scene, which clearly shows that men were
men in those days. The print shows the horses scampering
along just above the apparently sheer 1,000 foot drop into
Blea Water, and one can imagine the effort needed to get

all the impedimenta, including the barrels of beer, up the rough slopes on to the distant summit. What happened on wet, windy days one can only guess.

Right up to comparatively recent times the meet at the Dun Bull used to be quite a big occasion lasting, I think, two days even just before the demolition of the old inn. Joe Bowman used to lead the two days hunting by the Ullswater Hunt, and there were also hound trails, sheepdog trials and clay pigeon shooting. An old account of the proceedings states that after the hunting, the huntsmen, shepherds, visitors, sheepdogs and terriers, were admitted in the Dun Bull for a hearty meal, but the poor hounds which had been doing most of the work were not allowed inside. The appointed chairman sat at the head of the table, with the sheepdogs and terriers enjoying themselves underneath among the farmers' boots, and after the usual toasts the chairman would call for a song. In turn, everybody would have to sing at least one song, and the old account ends; 'Sometimes if a song has a good swing, the men get particularly enthusiastic, the shepherds beat on the tables with their sticks, and the sheepdogs and terriers join in the chorus with enthusiasm or execration, no man knows which'.

It is said that Joe Bowman could sing a hunting song at three o'clock in the morning and be out with his hounds, fresh as paint, before nine – but then Joe was an exceptional man. No doubt they will be singing the fine old hunting chorus 'Joe Bowman', at both Mardale and Troutbeck tomorrow in memory of a man who is much closer to Westmorland hunting than the legendary John Peel.

I hope to be able to attend the Troutbeck meet, which has now lost the services of old Sam Beaumont. In his quiet way, Sam ran this meet really well, and he certainly knew his job at the sheep pen. As the sheep were brought in from near and distant pastures, Swaledales, Herdwicks, half-breds, he would say with immediate authority – "Yon lot's Joe Tyson's from Kentmere", or, "Thems the two

Herdwicks as Ned Braithwaite lost in early summer" – and he was very rarely wrong. Sam, like most dales farmers, could have recognised his own sheep instantly, but he was quite remarkable in being able to recognise other sheep nearly as quickly. He will be missed at Troutbeck, but no doubt the tradition will be carried on by the other experts, Billy Leck and Billy Brownrigg.

The Coniston pack will be brought over to Troutbeck by Anthony Chapman this afternoon, and the hunt will set off, from behind the Queen's Head at 9a.m. tomorrow. There may be two days hunting in the valley later in the week, and tonight is the night of the Troutbeck Hunt Ball so it is a really important week for this little Westmorland village.

The number of sheep brought along to the shepherds' meets of today for exchange is not nearly so large as in former years but the method of identification is exactly the same. Each farm inherits its own ear marks, and it is believed this practice has descended from the Vikings to whom 'lug marks' were 'law marks'. If the ear is 'cropped' it means the end is chopped clean off, but it may also be 'forked' or 'ritted', which means slit down the centre. If they are 'fork-bitted' it means a V-shaped notch is cut out of the side of the ear, while 'key-bitted' means a square cut notch. Each ear has a 'top side' and a 'bottom side' and of course, each sheep has two ears, so that the number of combinations is very considerable.

In addition, there are the horn burns and the marks, sometimes different colours are used, on various parts of the body. Usually these are stripes, or 'pops', which means round blobs, or initials.

I believe *'The Shepherds' Book'*, compiled by J. Walker of Martindale in the beginning of the nineteenth century, was the first of the Lake District guides to catalogue all the different markings, and later on guides came out for each of the districts. Some of these books, hundreds of pages in size, had the marks, or 'smits' as they are called, coloured in red or black on engravings of page after page of prize sheep. Under each engraving was a description of the markings which would read something like this; 'Cropped and under key-bitted near, under halfed far, stroke from shoulder blade on near side over back, pop on tailhead'.

This may sound double Dutch to most people, but it is information of this sort which men like Sam Beaumont carry about in their head, just as you and I might remember telephone numbers. And tomorrow they'll get along alright at both Mardale and Troutbeck, without the need of a shepherds' guide.

AUTUMN ON PILLAR ROCK
9 October 1953

Officially, I suppose, the Lake District 'season' is over. Some of the hotels are already beginning to close down for the winter, the bus companies have finished with their summer timetables, the lake steamers are laid up, and small boys have already started collecting bonfire material. It has not been a good season. Some hotel keepers or caterers will tell you it has been the worst season they can remember, although others in the same village will admit that, on the whole, they have had a good summer. The trouble has been the constant wet weather and the only explanation I can give for the exceptional popularity of the Windermere steamers this summer is that, no doubt, it is possible to enjoy a sail on the lake when the day is too miserable for anything else.

The odd feature of our Lake District 'season' has always seemed to me to be the fact that our visitors so often see the district at its worst. Lakeland is much more beautiful in autumn or spring than in high summer, and the weather is so often better in April, May and October than in those notoriously wet months of July and August. The only thing wrong with these strangely unpopular holiday months is that the days are shorter, but even here it is possible to make adjustments. We can all remember October with weeks of dry cloudless skies with the colourings of the woods and the fells at their very best, the air bracing and the views, unspoilt by heat haze, strikingly clear.

Last Sunday was one of these days. It might not be a popular holiday month, but the sun was scorching hot in Mosedale, there was hardly a cloud in the sky all day, and although we had turned back the clocks the previous evening we were on the fells until seven o'clock and it was still light enough to see where we were going.

Two of us were taking a small son and a daughter, respectively, for their first visit to Pillar Rock. We did not leave Wasdale Head until noon but we were all on top of the Rock by three o'clock. There were several other people about us on the crag – the biggest precipice in the Lake District – but all were local climbers. Pillar Rock is a remarkable place for finding things. A few months ago I found a compass – which is still working – a few yards away from the vertical rift of Walker's Gully, and last Sunday my friend found a fine clasp knife on the Shamrock Traverse. Last Sunday also, the bowl of my pipe dropped 200 feet down the Old West Route, striking the rocks several times in its flight, and then bounded over the depths of Savage Gully. I went down for it and was remarkably lucky to find it still intact, although a little battered.

We stayed on top for at least an hour. It was warm, sunny and windless and the young fir trees in Ennerdale lay like a carpet more than 2,000 feet almost vertically below us. Every detail of the fells for many miles around was sharp and distinct, and when an aeroplane zoomed over us we could read its markings quite easily. A pair of ravens flew over the Rock, turning somersaults either to show off or because it was such a lovely day.

The summit of Pillar Rock is not really a good view point, however, so after we had climbed down we went up to the top of Pillar mountain, and then along to Wasdale by the ridge – possibly the most neglected fells in the Lake District. From near the ruined cairn on Pillar the view was as extensive and lovely as you can get anywhere in the Lake District. The towns along the West Cumberland coast were perfectly clear, with the shape of the Solway Firth drawn as if on a map, and the Scottish Lowland hills looking higher than they really are. Closer at hand the most striking features were the great precipices of Scafell Crag, lit by the evening sun; the extraordinary shape of Great Gable – probably the most easily recognisable mountain in the Lake District from any position; and the remarkable lighting of the Grasmoor range, making these modest fells look quite jagged and impressive.

Between us and Gable sprawled the great mass of Kirk Fell, one of the least photogenic of our Lakeland hills, for it looks so dull and uninteresting from all sides, but a good mountain from which to look out on to the surrounding hills. The tall chimneys of the atomic energy station at Sellafield were out of sight behind the foothills, but we could see the estuary at Ravenglass and the confluence there of the rivers Esk, Mite and Irt. The sun was just beginning to dip behind the western horizon and the sea was illuminated with a great golden band of light.

It was beginning to grow dark as we came down from the ridge and very soon we were sniffing the wood smoke at Wasdale Head, and a few moments later had reached the first lamp lit windows after a lovely October day.

THE MELTING MISTS
29 March 1957

One of the greatest sights ever seen by the man who wanders in the mountains, but never by the town dweller, is that of the sunshine chasing the mists from the fells. One moment, the traveller is in a dark, damp world with nothing to see but a few yards of swirling mist; the next, he is looking through a window in the clouds at sunlit fells perhaps 10 or 20 miles away.

It was like that last Sunday, from noon onwards one of the loveliest mountain days so far this year. I had arranged to meet two friends at Grisedale Tarn at noon, and left my car by the heap of stones at Dunmail Raise. This is still thought by some people to mark the last resting place of the last King of Cumbria, defeated hereabouts 1,000 years ago by Edmund of England. Without much enthusiasm I trudged through the mist up Raise Beck. When the boggy track petered out near the Willie Wife Moor visibility was no more than a yard or two and I had to set a compass course for the tarn. And believe it or not, I nearly walked into the tarn, so closely did its unruffled surface resemble the thick, clinging mist.

There was no sign of my friends by the cairn, near the waters edge, so I sat there and had my sandwiches while I thought of the strange story that the crown of King Dunmail (or Domnhall) was flung into the tarn after that battle of long ago. Once a year, so it is said, his warriors return to earth, lift the crown from the water and carry it down the gorge to the grave at Dunmail Raise. They strike the great pile of stones with their spears and three times the royal voice comes out of the tomb, "Not yet, my warriors, not yet." It is not yet the day for the king to arise from his long rest and reconquer Cumberland.

I am well aware that W. G. Collingwood wrote that King Dunmail lived thirty years after the battle and died on a pilgrimage to Rome, and that the romantic cairn on the top of the Raise was rebuilt by the Manchester navvies when Thirlmere became a reservoir. But sitting up there in the mist by the tarn on Sunday it was pleasant to imagine that a golden crown lay underneath the waters at my feet, and that perhaps the warriors might choose that very day for their return to earth.

When I had eaten my sandwiches and walked most of the way around the tarn I found my friends who, for half an hour, had been casting about in the mist for me, and we set off to investigate the recesses of a certain gully. And on the way there we saw the miracle of the melting mists – we see it perhaps two or three times every year but each time it seems new and miraculous. The complete transformation took no more than a minute. While stumbling, rather wet and cold, up slippery boulders, the mists were suddenly swept away and we saw the long length of Grisedale below us basking in the sunshine, blue skies, billowing white clouds and the water steaming off the rocks. The change could hardly have been in greater contrast, and the bright, sunny weather with its magnificent views remained with us all day.

Later, from the summit of Helvellyn we could see quite plainly to the northwest, the summit of Criffel in Scotland which is 40 miles away as the crow flies, and to the southeast, Ingleborough which is about the same distance away. We could also see everything in between which meant, in a sense, an 80 miles view. February and March are the months for these long views, in another month or two haze will prevent such clarity.

In the gully we had some fun with the dogs, my friends' large retriever and my own small border terrier. As a rock climb the gully does not rate very high and it was only after we had concluded certain other explorations that we decided we might as well continue up its rather loose and slimy interior. The retriever is a better climber than my dog, but when he is in difficulties he is not nearly so easy to handle. We got them up the first pitch by combined tactics with one man at the top, another halfway up and the third at the bottom. When the dogs were not being pushed to the extent of outstretched arms, or pulled vertically upwards by the scruff of the neck, they were able to scramble about fairly successfully on their own. The trouble was not so much on the pitches themselves, but on the steep, loose scree between pitches. Here the dogs were continually sending down loose chunks of rock, or starting minor avalanches, or getting mixed up in the rope. Their mountaineering technique left much to be desired.

The top pitch proved impossible for our crude push and pull methods, and we had to tie the animals on and climb the thing properly. We discovered that there is a right and a wrong way to tie a dog on to a rope after one of them had fallen out of his waist loop onto the head of the long suffering third-man. There had to be one loop tight around the chest and another, slacker, around the neck. In this way they were hauled up bodily like sacks of coal and did not appear at all concerned about swinging in mid-air.

We only saw one other person along the whole of the long summit ridge to Helvellyn, but any Sunday in August there will be scores of people up there. Helvellyn is perhaps the most visited mountain in the whole of Lakeland and it is a pity that its western slopes are so dull. But it makes up for this fault with the crags and ridges it sends down to the east.

There were still the remains of snow cornices up there and it was possible to stand knee deep in the stuff if you wished. From the top we could see the sun glinting like a heliograph on something about 3 miles away down Grisedale and knew, although we could not see it, that this was the windscreen of my friend's car. Almost every mountain in Lakeland, all the way around the compass could be clearly seen and it was strange that a wisp of cloud hung around the summit of Great Gable all day, but nowhere else.

I left my friends on the summit of Dollywaggon Pike and trotted due west down the hillside into the setting sun, while a pair of ravens lazily circled overhead. Earlier in the day we had twice seen a peregrine, perhaps the same one, but I will not now identify its crag in case it is a new one to the egg thieves.

And so ended another simple day in a familiar corner of the Lakeland fells. We had been on perhaps the most popular summit of all and had only seen one other person all day, apart from some distant dots on Fairfield. Many a weekend I do not see a soul. It simply underlines the old truth, the shortness of the Lakeland season. From October to May you can generally have the fells to yourself, and in my opinion this is the best half of the year.

STICKLE TARN
7 February 1958

One of the best known tarns in the whole of Lakeland – Stickle Tarn underneath the crags of Pavey Ark in the Langdale Pikes – may be changing its size and appearance in the not very distant future. I hear there is quite a chance it may become a natural tarn again. It may surprise some people to learn that Stickle Tarn is not a natural sheet of water, being in fact a reservoir, but it is even more surprising to trace how many of our lakes and tarns are (or have been) in commercial use, and have had their appearance altered in one way or another. Nobody is bothered very much by the fact that Stickle Tarn is a reservoir, and dozens of people pass along its shores each year without noticing the embankment. My only criticism of Stickle Tarn from an aesthetic point of view would be that a photograph taken from high up on Pavey Ark gives the tarn rather an ugly, square shape, but this is really only a quibble.

Of course, Stickle Tarn has not been in commercial use for many years. It was made into a reservoir for the former Elterwater gunpowder works in 1824, but these works were closed down years ago. An embankment of earth and stone walls was built on the glacial moraine separating the tarn from the steep drop down Mill Gill, and the tarn was thus deepened and enlarged. Now, discussions are to take place shortly to decide whether or not to breach the dam and allow the tarn to return to its former shape and appearance.

This would not be done, of course, in order to improve the scenery, but rather as an economic measure, since reservoirs are expensive things to maintain these days and their owners have important responsibilities – particularly from a safety point of view – towards the general public.

Writing of Mill Gill reminds me that the Ordnance Survey maps always call it Stickle Ghyll, which I am sure is wrong twice over. The local name – which should be the correct name – of the stream which comes out of Stickle Tarn is Mill Gill or Beck, and Millbeck is the name of the farm at the foot of the gill. Climbers and walkers always call it Mill Gill in their guides and so, I believe, does Bartholomew. The spelling 'ghyll' is an affectation, probably invented by Wordsworth. It is always applied to Dungeon Ghyll (and to the hotels there) and by long usage is probably correct by now, but applied elsewhere this spelling is, strictly speaking, incorrect. Stickle Ghyll and Stock Ghyll are, I believe, the only incorrect spellings perpetrated by the Ordnance Survey who are usually so accurate.

Many years ago, the farmhouse of Millbeck was probably the only place for refreshment in Langdale, or at any rate in the upper part of the dale. The road in those days lay around the back of what are now the old and new hotels and many a weary traveller from Borrowdale to Eskdale must have been glad to reach Millbeck for a meal and a drink.

Returning to Stickle Tarn, I wonder how many of my readers have noticed the very handsome cairn about halfway up the screes between the tarn and the foot of Pavey Ark. It is pretty well on the route taken to reach the foot of Jack's Rake. This cairn is one of the many little mysteries of the fells which have puzzled me for years. Set into the extremely well-built cairn, obviously a craftsman's job, is a smooth stone tablet which bears the initials 'JWS 1900'. Whether 'JWS' was the builder of the cairn or whether it commemorates him I cannot say. For all I know 'JWS' might have fallen to his death from the crag above and the cairn been built as his memorial. I have never seen the cairn mentioned in any guide book. Perhaps one of my readers could solve the mystery?

Another mystery about this part of the world is who was 'Jack' of Jack's Rake? As most of my readers know Jack's Rake is the easy scramble which starts at the foot of Pavey Ark at the right hand side and mounts gradually to the summit of the crag, crossing several of the climbs as it does so. Although it is not a perfectly easy route, it is not really for walkers, it is, in effect, a very easy rock climb and is classified as such. Walkers without any climbing experience might be affected by the exposure of the place and there have, in fact, been one or two fatal accidents there.

The first record of its ascent was in the 1870's by a Mr R. Pendlebury, but it is probable that shepherds had been up and down the place for generations before then. But whether 'Jack' was one of these early shepherds or whether he was the first man to spy out the route we will never know. We might just as well wonder how Harrison Stickle got its name or, for that matter, the derivation of the names of many of our mountains, fells and farms. What a pity that so much of this information has been lost forever.

I suppose the Langdale Pikes have been more thoroughly explored than any other part of the Lake District. To a climber the most interesting part of the Langdale Pikes is not the bold, craggy outlines of Harrison Stickle or Pike o' Stickle which look so impressive from afar, but become disappointing upon closer inspection, but rather the almost innocuous little fell of Loft Crag which lies between them. On the southwestern slopes of this otherwise uninteresting hill is Gimmer Crag – steep, beautifully clean rock, comparatively untouched by vegetation, and, in places as smooth as a church steeple. This is where some of the best climbing in Lakeland lies – a climbing ground discovered fifty years ago by men from Kendal, some of whom are still alive today. One of the early pioneers was Jonathan Staples, the Ambleside architect. One of the great advantages of climbing on Gimmer is that one is not constantly under observation from the road, which so frequently happens on some of the 'new' crags in this area, such as Raven Crag. Perhaps some of the newer generation of climbers enjoy being watched through field-glasses by people who have apparently driven into Langdale for this very purpose, but we of an older school prefer to get into the more remote crags for our exercise.

Perhaps the least visited of the Langdale Pikes is Thunacar Knott, which lies about half a mile west of Pavey Ark, and at a point where the county boundary takes a sudden dramatic turn. One of the interesting features of this little summit is that the cairn is not on the highest point but about 100 yards away.

Considering that the Langdale Pikes are perhaps the best known feature of the whole of the Lakeland hills, it is remarkable how little we know about them. Quite apart from Jack's Rake and 'JWS 1900' there is the interesting stone enclosure on the little used but delightful zigzag path which mounts from Mill Gill, behind Tarn Crag and on towards Blea Rigg. What was it used for? It is much bigger than any enclosure used by shepherds. And there are some curious shielings, low down and to the east of White Gill, which I have never been able to explain.

I have climbed on the various crags of the Langdale Pikes on scores of occasions and walked over the summits many dozens of times, but I still find it easy to get lost in thick mist on the high ground between High Raise and Harrison Stickle, and it is surprising to me there are not more accidents to walkers on these steep, rocky fells. Dungeon Ghyll itself can be a deathtrap to the inexperienced in bad weather. Maps and compasses are not the answer unless you really know how to use them. I remember one year when we were searching these fells in deep snow for two missing girl walkers (later found dead in Deepdale) meeting another party coming through the mist in exactly the opposite direction and making for the same rendezvous (the summit of Pavey Ark) as ourselves. They had turned around at their last stopping point, failed to take a proper compass bearing and, as a result were 180 degrees off course. And they were supposed to be experts.

Well, perhaps I have been turning in a circle since I started to write about Stickle Tarn, but don't blame me – blame my typewriter. Sometimes it just goes on and on.

BECALMED ON WINDERMERE
8 May 1959

There are few pleasanter ways of spending a lovely Lakeland evening than sailing a boat on Windermere, especially if you are doing so in competition with others. And many people – probably more than ever before – will be doing this from now on, for the Royal Windermere Yacht Club begin their season on Sunday, with nearly ninety craft listed on their books. Although I know one end of a boat from the other, and have crewed in yacht races on Windermere and in Walney Channel, I would not claim for one moment to be a yachtsman, I have, however, tasted the joys and the frustrations, and I well remember my last trip.

On a perfect evening we were practically becalmed in the middle of the lake. People on the shore would have been amused had they known we were racing, for in ten minutes we had hardly moved. We fussed with loose jib sheets, peered up anxiously at our limp racing flag, and prayed for a breath of wind. At least the skipper did. I was quite happy to smoke my pipe and take in the beauty of the scene.

On the skipper's instructions I had been dropping my matches overboard so that we could ascertain our movement, if any, but now he thought that the smoke from my pipe gave him a better indication of the direction of the wind. I was commanded to continue smoking. The smoke, he said, was much more useful than the motionless racing flag. Meanwhile, I sat and drank in the quiet loveliness of a Lakeland summer evening. The sun still blazed from a cloudless sky while the blue-lit fells, the woods along the shore and the trim lakeside lawns lay mirrored in magical perfection on the unrippled lake surface. Smoke from the houses hidden among the trees soared slowly and vertically and a fisherman, waiting for the evening rise, lolled, smoking in his boat, his straw hat over his eyes. And every now and again, 2 or 3 miles away up the lake, I could see the flashing white wake of a speedboat, noisily shattering the sleepy silence.

How long men have been messing about with sailing boats on Windermere nobody knows. As far back as 1818 regattas were being held, but I should guess that racing goes even further back than that. The present yacht club was founded in 1860 and received the Royal Warrant twenty-seven years later. Since then boat design has been constantly changing and so has the club itself. Nobody would have guessed, ten or twelve years ago that in 1959 half the boats in the club would be little GP 14's, and still less that the membership would include people with limited incomes who only wanted to join because they liked sailing. The popularity of the sport is now increasing rapidly among several new classes of society, not only on Windermere but on some of the other lakes as well.

Of course, an encounter with a gentleman in a jaunty nautical cap and blazer does not necessarily mean that you have met a member of the Royal Windermere Yacht Club. He might be a member of the Windermere Motorboat Racing Club, or indeed, of neither. It is interesting to notice how well these two clubs get on together for the only thing they have in common is a love of travel on water. They are complete opposites – the hare and the tortoise, the noisy and the silent, the internal combustion engine as against

Mother Nature's breezes, the grace and beauty of the swan compared with the sleek efficiency of the eel, and 'the fastest man in the world on water' and the slowest (my skipper and I). Yet each club keeps away when the other is racing, they share many facilities, they attend one another's dinners and they remain friends. Some people, I believe, belong to both clubs, although there are still yachtsmen of the old school who will tell you that they would not be seen dead in a motorboat, and keen, young speedboat enthusiasts who might look down their nose a bit at yachting.

The Royal Windermere Yacht Club will attain its centenary next year, but the motorboat club was only founded in 1925. The junior club can certainly claim however, that it is the premier club of its kind in the country while the Royal Windermere can nowadays do little more than point to its considerable age and most honourable traditions. A few years ago it used to claim to be the only yacht club proper in Britain racing on fresh water, but this is not now the case. One of the great achievements of the Royal Windermere was its introduction of the internationally known Windermere class of yacht, and they will I believe, tell you in the clubhouse that this is still the fastest yacht in the world for its size and type. They call these yachts '17-footers' but landlubbers should be told that this means 17 feet on the water line with an actual overall length of 25 feet 6 inches. They are of about 6 feet beam with a 4 feet draught, and have a sail area of 300 square feet. With the Langdale Pikes or the wooded shores as a background they make a most magnificent picture as they thread their way through the islands.

I see that twenty five of these 17-footers will be racing on Windermere this season, and almost all of these were built on the shores of the lake. Boat building is an old and honourable craft on the shores of Windermere and there are men still working today with half a century of solid experience behind them. Two of the principal firms are based on Bowness Bay and one of these built most of the 17-footers which will be racing this season. I used to believe that Windermere yachts were built very largely from the wood of the larch trees growing around or near the shores of the lake but nowadays, although the Windermere rowing boats used to be built entirely of local larch, this tree is now only used for a small part of the yacht building job. The planking most sought after in recent years has been mahogany from British Honduras, although African mahogany – not quite so suitable for freshwater – is sometimes used.

Yacht racing is a completely unpredictable sport. Windermere weather can be remarkably capricious and the result of a race can be in doubt until the very last moment. I have known three or four boats to be becalmed together when along comes a wind which sends one yacht nicely away, leaving the others immobile. Sudden squalls are another feature of Windermere and the small GP 14 dinghies can easily be overturned if handled incorrectly. In motorboat racing however – provided it is a non-handicap event – the craft with the most powerful engine, barring accidents, almost always wins.

The Windermere Motorboat Racing Club, with their close relations over many years with world record breaking have already started their season. This weekend the club hopes to welcome back to Lakeland their close friend, Mr Donald Campbell. Members of the club have been associated with him in all his record breaking and they will be with him again next week when he returns for further attempts – not on their lake but on adjoining Coniston Water.

AMONG THE CLOUDS
21 July 1961

On the last day of a holiday in the clouds two of us came sadly down from the snows, down through a long, deep valley carpeted with flowers and alive with the roar of white waters and the clink of cow-bells. I always feel a little sad when I come down from the mountains whether they are in the Alps or in Scotland or, just over the passes, in Cumberland, but since I am so very fond of Austria I felt particularly downcast last week. As I get older I prefer Austria to Switzerland. True, the mountains are not quite so high but the Austrian people, despite years of tragedy are friendlier and happier than the Swiss, their country less tourist-ridden and commercialised and the mountains less trammelled with tunnels, hydro-electric schemes, railways and ski lifts.

It's also cheaper in Austria and (dare I say it?) cleaner. I know all about the Swiss reputation for cleanliness, which is true of the cities and towns, but in Austria they are scrubbing out the mountain huts at four o'clock in the morning and the sugar for your morning coffee at 10,000 feet is separately wrapped, lump by lump. Even the cows look as if they have been washed.

Our only contact with shops, the tourist trade and modern civilisation was on the first and last days of the holiday. Throughout the rest of the time we were never lower than 8,000 feet above sea level and, most of the time, very much higher. We slept in mountain huts in great comfort which is a thing you cannot do in the huts of the Swiss, French or Italian Alpine Clubs. Here, you lie down jumbled together in straw or on boards with a score of other people of many nationalities, most of whom are either snoring or groaning. There is no air, for the windows are tightly fastened and from about midnight onwards people are getting up for their expeditions and clanking about the place in the incredibly noisy wooden sabots provided.

After a day or two of this one has to go down to the valley to buy food – and get some rest. But in Austria you can buy all your meals in the huts and get a good sleep every night. I slept soundly between sheets in each hut in a private room – rough and simple but spotlessly clean on every occasion – and it cost me about four shillings a night. This was the superior accommodation due to my years. My son, not so finicky, slept equally soundly but slightly more communally – and without sheets – in another room, for two shillings a night. One night he shared a room with two German doctors and a German parson so he was well provided for.

You've got to know the form about eating at these Austrian huts. If you are not careful you can spend a lot of money on such things as bread, butter, sugar, milk, tea and coffee. The thing to do is to carry up from the valley a long loaf about 2 feet long together with some butter, coffee, tea, a tube of milk, cheese and saccharine tablets. All you then have to buy for breakfast is hot water which might cost about a shilling. But this is much better than in the Swiss huts where you either have to pay for firewood or carry it up. If you don't take up a few simple requirements your hut breakfast, with each pat of butter, piece of bread and sugar added to the bill, will cost you much more than a continental breakfast should.

In the evenings you settle down to a good meal with a variety of soups, meat, ham, bacon, eggs, vegetables from which to choose, as well as those delightful jam omelettes and sometimes, luscious cakes with cream. To follow there are excellent wines and other beverages which will keep you going until the day's fresh air makes you drowsy for bed. I find I can live like a fighting cock, with all the food and drink I want, for a pound a day, and you could do it on less.

And there's no need to get up at midnight or two o'clock in the morning to climb mountains in Austria. Our earliest was four a.m. but we usually got up at five or even later. And since one goes to bed at ten o'clock this is no hardship whatsoever. Indeed, when the snowy peaks are flooded with the early morning sunlight it is difficult to stay in bed.

We climbed the highest peaks in the area, crossed many

glaciers and found many new friends – all of them Austrians and Germans. When I had trouble with my camera one German insisted on duplicating every colour shot he took so that he could send me along his slides for my own use. Another German insisted on sharing his food with me and later treating me to dinner because I had taken him up a climb. A third wanted me to stay for a fortnight's holiday at his home. We talked for hours together about the Berlin problem. "What a great tragedy," said one of them, "that our two countries should ever have fought each other." Each year I get letters and cards from Germans I have met in the mountains – all of them fine men, self-effacing, honest and sincere.

Many happy memories of Austria will help me through the English winter. I can look back on the views from half a dozen mountain tops, horizons of several countries notched by hundreds of snowy peaks with green valleys many thousands of feet below. We sat in the morning sunshine on these summits munching raisins or the traditional mint cake and trying to see how many distant peaks we could identify. Twice we saw eagles, but, surprisingly – for I have often seen them in other years – no chamois, and no marmots, either. Only mountain goats slithering down the lower crags.

We saw rock and snow avalanches – sufficiently far enough away to be interesting – and at our last hut, perched 10,000 feet up on a wild crag, nearly 5 inches of snow fell on our last night in the mountains and we awoke to a changed world. We crossed many fine glaciers and looked down many yawning crevasses into terrible, blue depths, cut our way up ice slopes in the morning sunlight, mounted rocky ridges and glissaded merrily down softening snow slopes in the early afternoon.

We saw mountain tarns the colour of the deep blue skies and other little lakes of the most vivid green, great ice pinnacles the size of churches, and waterfalls ten times bigger than the biggest in Lakeland. And when we went down to the huts or, at the end of the holiday down to the valleys, we crossed little green alps bright with bushes of alpenrosen, and here and there, spikes of purple gentian or cushions of moss campion. (The last time I had seen moss campion, I remembered, was just below the summit of Bidean, the highest mountain in Argyll.

Then down to the valleys, with little painted inns, the country folk in their national dress, the sheep, the goats and the cattle, all with their different sounding bells, the quaint onion-topped churches, the larch woods, the wooden houses with their flower-decked terraces, and, everywhere the familiar 'Gruss Gott' to the traveller down from the mountains.

Innsbruck is a fine town – one of the most splendidly situated in Europe – but it is a tourist town without the real Austrian flavour. To see the best of the real Austria you must penetrate into the least known valleys and, from them, climb past the chalets, the waterfalls, the flowering alps and upwards through the glaciers to the peaks among the clouds.

CHRISTMAS ON THE HILLS
3 January 1964

Twice during the Christmas period, I went up into the hills – alone, except for my dog, finding a great deal of beauty and exhilaration, but also several reminders that the Lakeland hills in winter must be respected if they are to be enjoyed. Both my simple expeditions were along the snow-covered Helvellyn range, possibly the most frequently trodden mountain area in England, but throughout the two days I saw only eight people in the hills – two on the first day and six on the second. However crowded our summer mountains may be, you can easily find solitude in the winter. Four days separated the two walks but the weather conditions were completely different on each occasion.

On the first day, I went up Striding Edge from Grisedale on a morning of low cloud with the snow-covered tops well hidden and a threat of bad weather on the way. Just before reaching the Edge we walked into a snowstorm, so that in a few minutes Sambo, my dog, was plastered white with snow. We kept on the top, going up and down all the little towers, until we came to the last one, where I had to let Sambo down into the gap on a length of nylon cord that I always carry for these occasions.

The scramble up to the top was interesting in the snow, but on the ridge there was almost a complete white-out so that some care was needed. Thick mist reduced visibility to a yard or two and, with everything covered in snow, it was not always easy to tell whether you were going up or down. You could just distinguish the slightly purer white of the edge of the cornice from the rest of the ridge and this provided the only sense of direction. This, regrettably, is strictly true for although I am always encouraging people to take a compass when going on the fells, I had stupidly left mine behind in the pocket of a second anorak discarded in the car. Having been up and over and along the Helvellyn range, winter and summer, on dozens of occasions, I thought I knew every inch of the ground but in a near white-out without a compass, this is just not good enough.

During the next hour or two I went along the range over Low Man and White Side to Raise, and then back again along Nethermost Pike to Dollywaggon, but twice I was completely lost and only found where I was by accident. There was never any real danger for I was equipped and fairly fit and the weather was not really cold, but it was easy to see how on a worse day a person with unsuitable clothing and limited experience of the fells could come to grief. As it was, I thoroughly enjoyed the experience and the little adventure made the day, as well as hammering home several old lessons. This was by no means the first time I have been lost in the fells – but there was no excuse for this one.

I met two other people on top, both lone walkers. One of them confessed he had been lost although using a compass. And when I had got below the mist and was picking my way down the icy Grisedale track at the end of the day, I reflected on the many possibilities – arrival in the wrong valley, remote from the car, for instance, or losing the dog – and concluded that once again I had had more good fortune than I deserved. And I mention the little incident now as a warning to others.

In contrast, the second trip was on a day of blue skies, hard snow and a biting wind. It was mild and thawing fast in Kendal with not a breath of wind to stir the trees, but you could nearly lean on the wind on the summit of Raise and the snow was so hard that a kick made no impression. The views were magnificent – warm golden browns, yellows and orange in the valley the beginnings of a splendid sunset in late afternoon, and sunlit snows both at our feet and on the tops of the distant Pennines. On the way up the steep snow-filled gully we call Savage's Drift, I found it convenient to cut steps with my ice axe. I could have avoided the steeper places and kicked my way up but it was more interesting to choose the more sporting way and get in a little practice.

And I was so interested that I must have forgotten poor Sambo who normally gets up steep snow better than a human being. At the foot of the slope he was close behind; when I looked down from the top he was far below our starting point and slowly coming up. And a lone skier at the top of the drift told me he had seen the little fellow slip out of his steps and slide on his back all the way to the bottom. He must have slipped about 400 feet, but when he eventually climbed up again he seemed none the worse. On the top of the mountain I noticed he had cut one of his pads and was leaving red footprints in the snow but this, I think, had been caused through the ice later on and quickly mended causing no trouble.

But if my dog could slip down this sort of slope, incredibly sure-footed as he is, how much easier for an ill-equipped and inexperienced walker to do the same – probably with much more serious consequences. I've rarely known the snow in Savage's Drift – or elsewhere in the hills for that matter – to be as hard as it was on Boxing Day. It was rock hard, for instance, on the top of White Side and, without an ice axe, the steeply-tilted track down into Keppel Cove would have been extremely difficult. Even Sambo had to slide nearly all the way down and more than once I wished I had brought my crampons along.

Two days therefore, each with their hidden menace – the thick mist and the snow on one occasion although a balmy day in the valley; and the ice hard snow on the second day of sunshine and thaw in the meadows. And yet there was a third day last weekend when we were skiing at nearly 3,000 feet – again in thick snow so soft that without skis you sank up to your knees.

NEAT CAIRNS ARE BEST
28 October 1966

On clear days, and especially when it's going to rain the next day, I can see from my windows the cairn on Thornthwaite Crag in the High Street range, 10 miles as the raven flies but a great deal further by any human route. And when I was standing by the cairn the other day I could, with difficulty, just pick out my house. I suppose this cairn is one of the finest in the district – it used to be a beacon many years ago – and it gives the mountain a distinction it might not otherwise enjoy. For although there are many finer mountains than Thornthwaite Crag there are not many better built cairns in the Lake District than this 14 feet high column of stones.

The one on the top of Pike o' Blisco, overlooking Langdale is a fine job – although sometimes mutilated by hooligans –

and Hallin Fell boasts a splendid edifice, obviously built by masons, but many of the others are very casual affairs indeed. The summit of Helvellyn, for instance, is simply crowned with an insignificant heap of stones, while Skiddaw, besides its bits of crude shelters, only has the Ordnance Survey's triangulation column to mark its summit, and the fine, shattered top of Bowfell is merely graced by the addition of a rough pile of boulders. Mind you, I am not calling for more and better cairns. There are already many more cairns in the Lake District mountains than we need, and most of them are in the wrong places. But it is curious that the size of the summit cairn has little or nothing to do with the importance of the mountain in Lakeland.

Cairn building in some parts of Tibet is almost an art – although the summits of Everest and the big Himalayan peaks are still undesecrated by man – but in Lakeland it can be a higgledy-piggledy business indeed. A few are the work of craftsmen, but most of them are not much more than tumbledown heaps, and some summits – like the top of Harter Fell in Westmorland – are marked with an ugly jumble of iron posts and railings.

I would say that the top of a mountain deserves a cairn, but my own preference is for no more than a reasonably neat heap of stones collected from the area around the summit. This is not to say that I disapprove of some of the well-built cairns which are well worth preserving as examples of craftsmanship, but I don't think these ornate affairs are really necessary. In a few cases the cairns are monuments and naturally these must be carefully maintained, but many of the unnecessary ones would be better flattened. Fairfield, for instance, has many cairns scattered across its broad summit and in mist this profusion can be most confusing. Ill Bell, too, has several quite well-built cairns scattered around its highest point – why I cannot imagine.

Some of our cairns, of course, are historic. These include the Westmorland Cairn built by the Westmorland brothers on the crags below the summit of Great Gable to mark the point from which they considered the finest view in Lakeland could be obtained. And they were not far wrong. Another historic cairn is the Robinson Cairn, marking the end of the High Level Route on the way to Pillar Rock, which is the memorial to John Wilson Robinson, the pioneer climber and fell-walker who died nearly sixty years ago.

Then there is the huge cairn on the summit of Scafell Pike, with its tablet commemorating the gift of the summit to the nation, and the cairn on the top of Great Gable, with its memorial to mountaineers killed in the First World War. Nobody, so far as I know, looks after these cairns, but they should not be allowed to fall into disrepair, as the one on Scafell Pike seems to be doing. This is an ugly affair, but it has its associations for many people, and it would be a pity if it was allowed to fall to pieces like the ruined heap on the top of Coniston Old Man.

But cairns falling to pieces is one thing, while cairns being deliberately pulled to bits is another. I have mentioned the damage to the fine cairn on Pike o' Blisco, but there has also been stupid destruction of cairns on Lingmell, Dale Head and other places. What these young hooligans hope to achieve by this sort of behaviour I cannot think. If it is to record their protest against cairns in general it has no effect, since the cairns are generally rebuilt into even more splendid erections. My own view is that these cairn destroyers are merely doing their senseless damage for the 'kick', and it's a great pity that the fells seem to attract a few of these people every year.

Some of our mountain tops are curious places. One of them, High Pike, near Caldbeck, used to have a shepherd's bothy on the very summit – the ruins are still there – and at one time there was also an iron garden seat up there, replaced a few years ago by a stone seat. Thunacar Knott has a tiny tarn on its summit and so has Red Screes, while Rest Dodd, above Hartsop, used to have a flagpole on its cairn. The top of Tarn Crag above Longsleddale has a survey post above a wooden platform – left by the Manchester Corporation engineers more than thirty years ago – and there are summits with no more indication than a wobbly iron post. Perhaps the variety of these summit adornments makes for interest and the average cairn is certainly a more welcome sight than the triangulation column seen on many tops.

My grumble, however, is not against summit cairns – provided there are not too many of them on each top – but about the completely unnecessary cairning of well-worn mountain tracks. Some of these track markings are important – the one, for instance, which indicates, in thick mist, where to leave the Bowfell track up The Band and turn right for Bowfell Buttress, or those on the Gavel Neese that mark the way to the Napes Ridges on Gable – but hundreds of others are merely annoying and nothing more than unsightly rubbish heaps. In places on rocky tracks, whitened by thousands of boot nails, you will find them every few yards. Properly sited cairns are of great help to the walker in mist, but when multiplied a hundred times they become not only useless but actually misleading. Big cairns are not required, for the fell-walker with his eyes about him should be able to read the message of the smallest heap of stones.

This is one of the attractions in walking in the Scottish Highlands; the tracks are generally few and far between, but here and there, just when you want it, you will find your cairn. It is surprising how small a cairn may be, and yet tell its message. The rock climber marks the beginning of a new climb with two or three stones laid together and the fell-walker should be able to manage with something similar. In the Isle of Skye where you can encounter some of the roughest country in Britain you will find few cairns, but they are all in the right places. As like or not the cairn will merely consist of three or four stones laid on top of a slab of rock, but this is quite enough to show the way. This, indeed, is surely the right way to mark the mountain routes – tiny heaps of stone in just the right places, rather than signposts or splashes of paint or scratchings on the rock.

By and large the tracks over the Lakeland fells are extremely well-marked, and there is much less need for cairns here than in other mountain areas in Britain. I wish we could start all over again by levelling out all the silly cairns on well-marked tracks and placing just a few small ones where they are really needed.

If the hooligans left the graceful summit cairns alone and turned their attention to the thousands of rubbish heaps – taking away the rubbish they found underneath them – we might be getting somewhere.

THE SECRET TARN
6 November 1970

The explorer travelling though the Himalayas, the wilds of Patagonia or Antarctic wastes can often discover mountains and valleys not marked on any map, but it may come as a surprise to some people that the same sort of thing may occasionally be possible in our little, over exposed Lake District. No mountain country in the world has been more thoroughly explored, mapped, written-up, photographed and argued over than our tiny 900 square miles of natural beauty, and yet even today you can still find places that the mapmakers have missed. Perhaps not mountain ranges – although some of our tops are still without a name, and some of the crags unmarked on the map. And certainly not valleys, although many important tracks are still missing. But scores of tarns, among the loveliest features of our mountains, are unrecorded.

Now, as far as the one-inch map is concerned this is understandable in the case of small sheets of water, although there is no real reason why they could not be included on the six-inch. But I have in mind fairly large tarns quite big enough to merit inclusion and in particular, one quite sizeable tarn which has never, to the best of my knowledge, ever appeared on any map – until now.

I have known this tarn for years and have always wondered why the Ordnance Survey men never found it, for it must be as big as Lingmoor Tarn and many times bigger than Hard Tarn in the Helvellyn range. It lies exactly on the Westmorland – Cumberland boundary, which many mapmakers must have walked over the years, about midway between Steel Fell and Calf Crag and just above the 1,500 feet contour. Of irregular shape, it squats on the ridge at the head of the Greenburn valley and it must be at least 100 yards long. Nearby is another tarn, about half its size, and some distance away there are two or three smaller pools. But for the past 200 years or so of reasonably accurate mapmaking, all have remained unnamed and undiscovered.

The absence of the tarns from the maps must have worried walkers over the years, for if you stumble in the mist on to a fair-sized tarn that is not on the map you begin to wonder whether you are off route. I happened to be walking these fells recently in thick mist, relying on map and compass, and was puzzled by the tarn, until I remembered it was the unnamed tarn I had often seen from the surrounding heights. It is not a particularly exciting tarn but it shows up well from the ridge leading up to Ullscarf – a much bigger stretch of water than the tarns on Greenup Edge that are marked on the map.

I decided to see if I could trace any reference to the Steel Fell tarn when I got home and found that both Wainwright and Heaton Cooper had found the tarn, but had failed to find any name or any mention, even on the six-inch map. Heaton Cooper suggests the name Steel Fell Tarn and estimates its surface area as about 40,000 square feet. I would have thought it was rather more. And then out of curiosity I decided to have a look at my brand new one-inch Ordnance Survey map – the one with the new levelling that dared to chop several feet off Scafell Pike and our other main tops – and found that they have discovered the tarn at last. On my recent walk I had carried my usual dog-eared map – the edition before the latest – since the new map seemed too new and crisp to use on a wet, misty day and I was delighted to find that justice has now been done – except that the tarn is still nameless.

I suggest that they call the 'new' tarn, Steel Fell Tarn as named by Heaton Cooper, or if they prefer it Boundary Tarn, since the county boundary seems to go right through it, with half in each county.

This country around Wythburn is among the least visited in Lakeland, particularly on the north side of the dale. On this last outing I went right around all the tops enclosing the valley and only saw two people all day. The steep slog in thick mist up Steel Fell from the top of Dunmail Raise was not particularly rewarding except when the mists parted for a moment to reveal the top of Dollywaggon Pike, apparently floating in the sky. As I scrambled higher the cars going over the pass shrank smaller and smaller and their noise gradually decreased, until I topped the ridge when it stopped altogether, and I was alone in the mist amidst the silence of the fells.

I passed the nameless tarn, went over Calf Crag, and then crossed from Westmorland into Cumberland at the curious stile across the track for Greenup Edge. All the posts that marked the county boundary have long since disappeared but the stile remains, looking oddly forlorn. I continued over High Raise and then over the lonely mountain of Ullscarf, where hardly anybody ever goes. On the way up the ridge the mist lifted and I saw the tarn again – the only sheet of water to be seen.

From the top of the mountain it proved quite an interesting expedition to steer a compass course straight for Steel End across the rocky little valleys that lie in between. It brought me out on the top of Nab Crags with a scrambling descent into Wythburn after a remarkably unusual view of Thirlmere and the Helvellyn range. From this rocky perch there is a refreshing feeling of height and space, after so much slogging over rather dreary grass slopes. The intake fields of Wythburn looked vertically below and Helvellyn seemed to soar into the clouds above the lake much more impressively than when seen from the valley. This is the sort of reward the lone walker can often win on a dull, misty day – to top a ridge and suddenly see the world open up below his feet, perhaps right across the dale to the skyline.

Mist in the fells can hide the dull places and provide magic casements through which one can look out on to more exciting bits of upland landscape. Impenetrable mist on the fells is rare. Sooner or later the curtains are torn away – often very quickly on a windy day – and suddenly a triangle of blue sky or a glint of sunlight on a distant crag, make it all worthwhile.

A LOOK AT THE ROCKIES
9 August 1974

We drove eastwards into the mountains with the morning mists rising through the forests and the sunshine sparkling on remote, snow-capped peaks, a vertical mile above the road. These were the Selkirks – bold, craggy mountains with steeply-tilted glaciers – and, beyond Rogers Pass, we looked across to the Rockies – the exciting 1,000 miles long frontier between British Columbia and Alberta. Our daughter drove the 700 miles from Vancouver to Calgary in two days but I was allowed three days at Lake Louise in which to explore the Rockies. You could climb there for three months and still only scratch the surface but at least I was able to get the feel of the Rockies, and to see some of their tremendous scope, grandeur and beauty.

Our first sight of one of 'the world's great views' – of the turquoise waters of Lake Louise glinting in the sunshine with the glaciers and the snow mountains behind – was somewhat marred by the serried ranks of parked cars and the camera-laden crowds in the foreground. All nationalities were among the tourist, but mostly coach-borne Americans – 'doing the Rockies' from the lawns and gardens of Chateau Lake Louise.

Without a climbing companion and with guides only available – at exorbitant cost – from Banff nearly 50 miles away, I went one day up to the glaciers of Mount Victoria, ascending a long snow couloir and scrambling up a little crag of rather loose rock. From our highest point – about 9,000 feet – I looked across at Abbot Pass and the serrated summit ridge of Mount Victoria, down to the Plain of the Six Glaciers, and over a sea of snowbound peaks that stretched north and south to seemingly limitless horizons. It was a day in a thousand – blue skies, crisp snows and fantastic visibility – and when I returned, hours later, along the lake shore, the crowds had gone and something of the peace of Lake Louise, before the tourist invasion, could be sensed.

You pay to drive into the Canadian national parks, Glacier, Yoho, Kootenay, Banff and Jasper – but nobody grumbles, for here is some of the best scenery in the world, and they look after it with a fierce pride. For my two expeditions into the mountains, I had to register, giving all particulars, and also report my safe return. The parks are run by wardens who are policemen, climbers, mountain rescue personnel and wildlife experts all rolled into one. From the chief warden of the area – Jim Rimmer, parachutist, mountaineer and trapper I was given much friendly advice and the loan of an ice axe and rope. Some of his advice was about how to cope with bears encountered in the mountains – a genuine hazard in these parts – but all I could do was to hope I did not meet one.

After my return from the Mount Victoria glaciers, Jim took me into the woods behind the Chateau late at night to meet a black bear he had seen an hour or two earlier, but we were unlucky and only saw his paw scratches on the hotel's garbage tanks.

My second modest expedition was a solo attempt on Mount Temple, at 11,635 feet the highest peak in the area, but this failed through heavy rain and thick cloud. I got onto the rock ridge of the mountain at about 10,000 feet but below the summit ice cap, and then decided – the weather conditions being miserable and the mountain rescue service an unknown quantity – to come down to Moraine Lake and the spectacular Valley of the Ten Peaks.

From above the top of Sentinel Pass, I had seen the clouds swirling around jagged rock peaks, looking rather like the Black Cuillin in Skye but nearly four times as high and, although I missed my peak and got very wet indeed, it had been an exciting day. On the way up I met three other climbers who had abandoned the peak on the pass so, having got higher, I felt reasonably content. These were the only genuine climbers I had encountered in all my mountain wanderings in Canada. Mountaineering in Canada does not seem to have the following, comparatively speaking, it has in Britain and you can't buy or hire an ice axe, rope, crampons or any other mountain equipment in Lake Louise, which is surrounded by magnificent mountains.

Banff is different but we could only spend a short day there – much of it in the palatial Banff Springs Hotel where we drank coffee on the terrace above the swimming pool in our old clothes and tried to work out if we had enough dollars to pay for a meal; but we hadn't. Earlier we had lazed at the Chateau Lake Louise where the cost of an 'ordinary' room, without dinner or breakfast for one night was $45 – about £20. Needless to say, we slept elsewhere.

As a mountaineer, the Rockies were, for me, the highlight of the holiday, although, through lack of a climbing companion, comparatively little was achieved. But, throughout our stay in Canada, I was impressed by the friendliness of the people, the tremendous scale of the country, its unexplored potential, the superb buildings in the cities and the pride that Canadians so rightly feel in their young country, with its short but exciting history. There is still a pioneering spirit in the country. You can find it in the little shack towns and even in the cities like Calgary which, with nearly half a million inhabitants, still looks unfinished.

Canada has the size and the natural resources and the drive among its people to become one of the great countries of the world – if it had really imaginative leadership. I have not seen so much of the prairies and nothing of the eastern part of the country, but I think I have seen some of the best of the west and can understand why so many British people have decided to make their homes out there.

And so I will always remember the beautiful city of Vancouver with its elegant skyscrapers, splendid parks, superb beaches and feeling for history, the snow-covered mountains and the still unexplored Indian country to the north, the grandeur of the Fraser Canyon, the long drive through the mountains to the rim of the Pacific, the great lakes and the neat little country towns and our morning sight of cloud-wreathed peaks from Rogers Pass.

Soon I will forget the complexity of the traffic, the soaring prices, the often humid heat, the lukewarm tea and the unexciting ice-cold beer.

Our last view of the Rockies from Calgary – a blue switchback along the horizon, 100 miles away – was a very sad moment, but our adventures were not yet over. Two hours delay at the airport through engine trouble and then, somewhere over Greenland, the announcement from the pilot that he didn't think he had enough fuel to reach Amsterdam. (There had been trouble refuelling at Calgary because of the great heat). He would have to come down to refuel in Scotland – at Prestwick. My car was in Manchester but, although I argued for half an hour, we were not allowed to fly there direct from Scotland but had to fly to Amsterdam – more or less over my house – and then back to Manchester.

They gave us a free lunch in Holland but we were seven hours late in reaching Ringway – at the same time as another plane reported to be carrying a bomb. We knew nothing about this until the following morning, although we had noticed some unusual police activity at the airport. Oddly, after all the careful screenings and checkings at foreign airports, we were allowed into Britain without even a glance at our cases or any signs of a customs check.

And then, back to driving on the left hand side of the road again and our first sight of the friendly Lakeland fells for a month.

PART TWO

Cumbria articles

LANTY SLEE
July 1953

We found Lanty's hideout by slithering down to the lowest tunnelling in the deserted quarry high above Langdale, wriggling through a hole and dropping 10 feet into the darkness. In five minutes our torches had shown us the whole story. There, close to the cave entrance, was the spring for his water, close behind on a platform of rocks was where he placed his still and underneath were the ashes from his scores of fires. Other discoveries came quickly – bits of rusted barrel hoops, a piece of piping which led to his 'worm' or perhaps carried away the exhaust steam, the store cupboard for his kegs, cunningly concealed by slates, and, among the ashes, part of an old clay pipe. We could imagine the old rascal sitting down there in the darkness more than a hundred years ago, watching his brew, smoking his pipe and listening. Listening for the tell-tale slither of scree which might mean the approach of the exciseman.

But no exciseman ever caught him here, for you cannot easily pick out a puff of steam on a wild hillside at night, and that was all Lanty ever gave away. He would steal through the deserted village after dark, cross by the Slater's Bridge, edge his way past the lonely tarn, and then climb up the steep, familiar fellside through the birches and the mountain ash, in and out of the great quarry hole, until he reached his eyrie under the crags of Wetherlam. A last look round to make sure he was not being watched, a pause to listen whether the 'gentlemen' were creeping up behind him, and Lanty would go to earth like a ferret.

It would be too dark to see The Road but Lanty knew exactly where it lay just 2 miles away to the northwest – the Smugglers' Road over Wrynose, a narrow, winding, exciting track creeping over the fells, past the Three Shire Stone to Ravenglass and the sea. No man knew The Road better than Lanty. Along this wild highway, on many a rough night, went Lanty's best in bottles and bladders – good, strong stuff for the gentry at ten shillings a gallon. And the feet of the ponies as they went trotting through the dark were bound with straw and the smugglers wore sacking on their shoes. More than once the dalesmen were ambushed by the excisemen, and there would be fights and scuffles in the mist, with a pistol shot echoing across the fells, a body slumped in the bracken, a few broken heads and no questions asked in the morning.

Another time the dalesmen might be luckier. Somewhere, high up among the rocks, Lanty's dog would suddenly sit up, ears well back, nose pointed into the biting wind whistling over the pass. "There's summat up," whispered Lanty, "luk sharp and git in amang them staens." And sure enough there would be the excisemen, hooded against the cold, riding up through the mist and over the top like shadows, their bridles jingling, while Lanty and his men lay with their faces in the ling.

It is just a hundred years since Lanty was caught, his still seized, and the old reprobate hauled protesting before the Hawkshead bench, so it was quite a coincidence that we should recently discover his least known and least accessible headquarters. All we had to go on was the vague description of an old dalesman who thought he remembered being shown the cave when he was a boy. Long before Lanty selected the spot the quarrymen had deserted the quarry and left it for the foxes, the owls, the rowan and the maidenhair fern, and the smuggler chose the darkest and most subterranean corner for his 'worm'. And not content with that he built a rough wall across the adit mouth, leaving only a 2 foot hole for wriggling through.

This then was where the only Lake District distiller and smuggler who has any chance of going down in history carried on his personal objection to the Distillery Act of 1834, although he had other, more accessible, headquarters. There was, for example, the still hidden under the flags of his kitchen at Low Arnside Farm, with a long pipe, cunningly contrived, to carry the exhaust steam out of the house and into a hedge in an adjoining field. Here was the ideal spot, for Lanty could pick out the excisemen riding along the road below long before they could even see the farm, and in a trice the evidence could be hidden and Lanty would become a simple farmer again.

Then there was another site hidden among the birches in Atkinson Coppice reached by swinging down a hole among the rocks on a long rope, and even after his last conviction when he became 'respectable' again it is said he had a crude distillery near the shore of lonely Red Tarn, a mile above the Three Shire Stone and nearly 2,000 feet up. But this was perhaps just for his friends.

The discerning gentry of the dales – among them, no doubt, the magistrates who sat in judgement upon him – were included among his customers but you did not get a bottle unless you knew the ropes. The drill was first to enquire of Lanty whether he had had 'a good crop of taties this year'. Once you were across this hurdle he might be ready to talk business.

But most of the stuff – and they say the old sinner made remarkably good liquor indeed – went over The Road, that ancient highway more than 2,000 years old where the Roman legionaries marched and the Viking settlers held their Parliaments. Here, on many a black night, Lanty and his confederates would meet, dropping down the pass into Westmorland, caravans of ponies laden with fresh salmon, great sacks of it, poached from the Duddon, and other illicit cargoes run ashore under the rocks of St Bees Head, the previous night. For whisky was not the only contraband which came over the fells. No doubt, too, Lanty, the rough Westmorland dalesman, would know all about the running sea fights with the Government sloops from Silloth and Annan or the Revenue cutter from Whitehaven, and many another dark adventure which could never be told. So his old clay pipe will remain on my desk.

A FAMILY ON THE CRAGS
February 1960

The Cumbrian who, with his brother, gave his name to the Westmorland Cairn on Great Gable – from which point of vantage they considered the finest view in all Lakeland could be obtained – died just fifty years ago. And now, with fitting timing, a cragsman's climb on Dove Crag, Patterdale, one of the steepest cliffs in England, has just been renamed Westmorland's Route in honour of his son – Lieutenant-Colonel Horace Westmorland of Threlkeld, surely one of the sprightliest septuagenarians in Lakeland, or anywhere else, today.

Although Colonel Westmorland – 'Rusty' to a host of climbers and skiers all over Britain and in many places abroad – has been climbing rocks for sixty years he is still able to tackle some of the harder routes and, only a short time ago, led his party of youngsters up a 'very severe' in his beloved Borrowdale. He would climb every day if he could find the companions; as it is, he has to content himself with three or four days a week in summer, and perhaps only a paltry two or three in winter. Only the mountains count; one can easily imagine him sulking in cities.

At seventy-three years of age 'Rusty' Westmorland is not only an extremely good rock climber and competent skier, but also manages, with or without conscious effort, to look the part. To many people, unfamiliar with the mountain scene, he must represent exactly their idea of the bold cragsman, bursting with health and determination. The clipped moustache, the erect bearing, the polished boots, and the neat, efficient clothes reflect his military background, while the tanned face, the clear, twinkling eyes, the jaunty Austrian hat, and the springy step suggest the mountaineer. The Mountain Rescue flash on his shoulder – he it was who revived the Keswick Mountain Rescue Team several years ago – is worn for use, not for ornament, and his general neat, well-groomed appearance on a climb is in striking contrast to that of the many dirty, bearded youths, clanking with ironmongery, who often decorate the crags today.

The yeomen forebears of Horace Westmorland farmed at Milburn under the shadow of Cross Fell – they had taken their name from their native county – but Rusty himself was born at Penrith, just over the Cumberland border, where his father had a leather business. Right from his birth the mountains were in his blood. His father, Tom Westmorland, his uncle Ned and his aunts were scrambling and camping in the Lakeland fells last century long before the joys of steep, remote places had become as commonplace as they are today.

One of his aunts – Mary (May) Westmorland – was the second woman to reach the summit of Pillar Rock, on 24 July 1873, the first having been a Miss A. Barker who had achieved the feat just three years earlier. May went up, unroped, with her brothers Tom and Edward and, on the summit, where they found a bottle containing the names of ten previous conquerors, they stood to attention and proudly sang *God Save the Queen*. Later Tom celebrated the occasion with a poem, *A Summer Ramble*, which describes the day in detail. A photograph taken at the time shows May to have been a short, sturdy, good-looking girl and her brothers to have been most determined looking men, sprouting youthful beards. May wore a smart, close fitting jacket, a short skirt and trousers rather like plus-fours, with collar and bow tie and a peculiar hat, not unlike a sailor's. Her brothers wore the outdoor clothes of the period and heavy shepherds' boots, and all three carried poles at least 6 feet long.

Another memorable day for the Westmorland brothers was when they skated the full length of Ullswater from Pooley Bridge to Patterdale and back to Watermillock, but the day they put their name on the map was a summer afternoon in 1876 when they built the Westmorland Cairn on Great Gable. They were not bad judges, too, for the sight of the patchwork fields of Wasdale Head nearly 3,000 feet below, the ring of the highest mountains in Lakeland all around, with Wastwater flanked by the frowning Screes, and the sea in the distance, is always a most memorable picture. Today the precipice below the cairn also bears the name of Westmorland Crags, and a rock climbing route up the centre is called Westmorland Ridge.

This was young Horace's legacy and he made full use of it. At eight years of age he went up Cross Fell, the great, sprawling Pennines peak above the home of his ancestors and later the same year we find him scrambling along Striding Edge. Each summer after that he and his friends scrambled, camped, rowed, sailed and walked the fells, and when he was eleven years of age the boy first saw and met real climbers – with ropes. They were a formidable party; Haskett-Smith, the first man to climb Napes Needle; John Wilson Robinson, the Cumbrian whose memorial is the cairn on the High Level Route to Pillar; and Geoffrey Hastings and Ellis Carr, two very prominent mountaineers.

As a boy of fifteen young Horace was taken by his father to the summit of Pillar Rock by way of the easy Slab and Notch route, and exactly fifty years later, in 1951, Colonel Westmorland achieved his great ambition by making a jubilee ascent of the Rock. The route chosen on this occasion was the considerably harder North Climb which Rusty, then sixty-five years of age, led throughout without any difficulty whatever, the event being fittingly celebrated on the summit with a bottle of wine.

Since that day, eight years ago, the old warrior, who looks no more than a cheery sixty, seems to have been climbing increasingly harder things, to the frequent embarrassment and shame of companions only half his age. And yet, fifteen years ago, this same man, after thirty-one years of service in the Canadian Army and half a lifetime of surveying, climbing and skiing in the Rockies and other exciting places, had been invalided home to England, and told to take things easy in his retirement.

Already his remarkable fitness is becoming legendary – that, and his gallant penchant for the company of young lady climbers – and his affection for steep rocks remains unabated. "The weather doesn't bother me," he told me the other day, "and I don't mind steep, exposed stuff on tiny holds. But I don't like too many of these arm pulls. Overhangs seem to be harder these days."

HARTER FELL
September 1962

When Helvellyn, Gable and the Langdale Pikes are swarming with people and cars are grinding over Hardknott Pass in scores you will probably find Harter Fell deserted except for the sheep and, perhaps, the buzzards flying overhead, for this little mountain, comfortably tucked between Eskdale and Dunnerdale, has never, to my delight, been a particularly popular shrine. Thousands drive over the pass within 900 feet of its summit each year and perhaps hundreds walk along the track across its western flank, but relatively few scramble to its three-pronged top and the fell is pleasantly free of highways, cairns, rusty tins and orange peel. Harter Fell, despite the prolonged activities of the foresters on its eastern and southern slopes, is a lovely little mountain and a fine viewpoint – a compact, knobbly mass of volcanic rock, splashed with bracken and heather, and nowadays, most nobly ringed with trees. Only a little hill as British mountains go but an upland of character with a niche in history.

Long before the Normans there was some sort of fort at Castle How, on its northeastern skirts, and for nearly 2,000 years the summit has looked down on Hardknott Fort, just over a mile to the north. Almost certainly the Romans or their legionaries will have scrambled to the craggy top where the Ordnance Survey have their triangulation column, and looked out over the Scafells or westwards down Eskdale to the sea.

Harter Fell may be said to belong to both the Esk and the Duddon since it feeds both rivers, but for me it has always been a hill in Dunnerdale – the best hill in Dunnerdale. Mostly, it has been the perfect hill for a summer evening before the sun dips below the summit – low enough to run up and down after tea with a bathe in the glorious pool at Birks Bridge to round off the day, and ideal for an evening scramble on the crags above the loop in the river. Sometimes we used to take a rope and, avoiding the fellside as much as possible, try to pick out a rock route all the way to the summit.

Other memories of more than thirty years ago are of walking over the shoulder of the mountain, laden with rucksack and tent, on our way to and from Wasdale Head. We used to go this way from Torver, or even Woodland or Foxfield, thinking little of it. Many a time I've come down in the darkness from Grassguards to the stepping stones across the Duddon.

The last time I was on Harter Fell, earlier this year, I had seen no-one on the mountain all day until coming down to Birks in the evening. On one of the lower cliffs a cragfast sheep was bleating piteously and I worked my way across to see what I could do, although I carried no rope on this occasion and was encumbered with a dog. But strangely enough the only people I saw in the valley that day were climbing on this little visited crag and, by a coincidence, I knew them. When I told them about the sheep some distance above them and to the left the leader went up to organise its rescue, but no sooner had he poked his face around the corner of the ledge on which she was marooned than the old ewe took her courage in both hands and leaped and scrabbled towards safety. She must have been on the ledge for at least a week for every scrap of herbage had been consumed or scratched away but it had taken a strange human face to frighten her into making the move she had been toying with for days.

The top of Harter Fell is an attractive place, quite craggy, with the actual summit rather higher than the Ordnance Survey column, a magnificent view of the Scafells 5 miles away to the north, and a bird's eye picture of Hardknott Fort. Thousands of people drive over the pass each year without noticing the fort, and even from inside the ruins its square shape is not apparent. But from the summit rocks of Harter Fell it stands out – thanks to the labours of the Office of Works – like a town on a map, and must be more visible nowadays than it has been for hundreds of years. You can see where the commandant's house stood, the headquarters block, the granaries and the baths, but you have to know where to look to spot the parade ground – about 300 yards away to the east on a slightly higher shelf. Here, nearly 2,000 years ago about 500 levies from Spain, France and parts of central Europe were licked into shape by Roman centurions, and here, for upwards of a century, they watched the road through the mountains and down to the sea.

Harter Fell is not the same mountain I knew as a boy but it has by no means been ruined by the Forestry Commission. It is part of their Hardknott Forest Park formed nearly twenty years ago and embracing 7,275 acres between Esk Hause in the north and Grassgarths in Dunnerdale to the south, and from Wha House in Eskdale over the passes to the Three Shire Stone. This is among the finest mountain country in Britain, but only about one quarter of the area is plantable – you can't grow conifers on crags and scree – and much of the suitable land in Moasdale and Wrynose Bottom has been acquired by the National Trust since the Park was formed. All that remains for afforestation are something like 1,300 acres around the lower slopes of Harter Fell and I understand that the present limits of the Commission's operations represent their planting boundaries. Upper Eskdale will never be planted with conifers nor will any more of the central valley heads. And nowhere will the conifers march above the 1,500 feet contour.

It is the way the Forestry Commission have gone about their job on Harter Fell that I find so encouraging. The regimentation you see elsewhere in Lakeland has been avoided as much as possible, while skylines have been left clear, and hardwoods liberally planted among the conifers. Sitka and Norway spruce may not be indigenous trees, but neither is the larch which Wordsworth found so offensive but which we now admire as one of our own, like the oak, ash and rowan. The evergreen spruces are also lovely trees – the Norway, with its blunt, dark green needles and the Sitka, almost blue green or silvery. And with the spruces the Commission have planted on the slopes of Harter many thousands of larches and pines – European larch and Japanese larch and the magnificent Scots pine – as well as the broadleaved hardwoods. There is beech, red oak and Norway maple, besides Lakeland rowans and birches, so that the woodlands mostly appear charming and colourful. The beech, in particular is a most colourful tree – russet throughout the winter, pale green in spring, a deeper green in summer and then the full glory of its autumn beauty. And the yellowish green of the Norway maple glows like patches of sunlight among the darker greens of the conifers.

But despite the new forests the walker has been left his paths and while one can hardly now wander at will you may reach the summit by a variety of routes. A glance at the map gives no clue to the attractiveness of the mountain – a dull rounded cone, you might think, ringed with circular contours – but in this case the map is wrong, or at least misleading.

For Harter Fell is very much a worthwhile mountain – splendidly alive with colour and shape. A mountain which will take the proposed forestry road through the conifers in its stride, swallowing it up without a murmur. A proud, handsome little fell, good to look at and superb to look from.

CARROCK FELL
October 1962

To reach the 'Back o' Skiddaw' country by road from the south or east you will probably outflank the Blencathra range, go through the sleepy little hamlet of Mungrisdale and on to Hesket Newmarket and a different sort of scenery. About a mile or so beyond the hamlet you cross the Caldew and embark upon a delightful unfenced road used as much by sheep as by motorcars. On your left is a tumbled, boulder strewn slope, studded with juniper and gorse, and the unseen summit above is that of the modest, little mountain of Carrock Fell.

Here is no fine peak, guarded by great crags and buttressed by soaring ridges, but none the less it is a fell with some character and rare individuality. For where else in Lakeland is there a mountain with an ancient hill fort on its very summit, and where else in these parts can you climb on gabbro – the wonderful rough rock of which the Black Cuillin of Skye is made? Indeed, they say that Carrock Fell contains more varieties of rock than almost any other height in England, which may or may not be true. Certainly, its southern slopes carry some of the most colourful patches of purple heather in Lakeland, while you can find white heather there much easier than in many parts of the Highlands.

Carrock Fell is an ideal place to visit when the mists are down on the higher fells, or for a short day, or for a bit of amateur geology or perhaps for a picnic with the children. Just the place for the antiquarian, too. Mostly, however, I have visited Carrock for the climbing – and found the short climbs unexpectedly difficult and much harder than those of equivalent standard in the Cuillin. We've generally gone on to the summit, or pottered around trying to find old settlements, interesting mine shafts or rare lumps of rock. For they tell me that even uranium can exist in some of the minerals found on Carrock Fell and the area has certainly been mined for wolfram.

You rarely find honest-to-goodness fell-walkers on Carrock. If you see anybody at all they will probably either be climbers trying to identify the rather disappointing little climbs, geologists with hammers, mineralogists or antiquarians. And I once met three young men in the higher crags erecting a hide for bird photography.

The ruins of the ancient fort on the summit are remarkable. They look like a tumble of large scree, draped in necklace fashion around the highest point. They cannot be scree because there are no crags above, and no scree is ever composed of such equally sized boulders. Many, many centuries ago – I don't think the exact age of the fort has ever been established – men carried these thousands of stones to the summit or dug them out of the ground and built their fort, no doubt as a look-out over northern Lakeland. Fragments of the original masonry still remain and the ring is broken in several places where perhaps there were gateways. Some distance away from the summit is an elaborate sheepfold built of the roughly dressed stones from the wall.

The ruined fort is not the only sign of man's work on Carrock, for on many parts of the fell there are tumuli, artificial mounds, piles of stones, short stretches of wall and sheep bields built perhaps from the collapsed ruins. Archaeologists have not yet pieced together the whole story of this strange little mountain but it seems likely that the early British knew the place and even lived on these heathery slopes above the Caldew. After the earliest settlers or soldiers

– perhaps hundreds of years later – came the miners, for down the centuries the fell has been excavated for many minerals, some of them rare. Mineralogists still visit Carrock Mine, more than a mile west of the summit, where wolfram was being worked not so very long ago. There are other mines not far away, including Carrock End Mine, near the road at the foot of the craggy eastern slope, and old miners' trods and the remains of watercourses.

All this activity stems from the fact that Carrock Fell is a geological mix-up, due to the sudden ending of the Skiddaw slate area and its junction with many different series of volcanic rocks. Geologists can explain this curious mixture, laid down perhaps millions of years apart but the average visitor can only marvel at the presence of so many different types of rock, sometimes within the space of a yard or so. I've seen lumps of gabbro, granite, slate of various kinds, and hard, volcanic rock on the same part of the fell, each with their attendant beds of scree and, perhaps not far away, a shining heap of some mica-like substance. And beneath these piled boulders and jumbled crags the foxes have their borrans – as safe as any in Lakeland.

From the summit you can see the Scottish lowland hills beyond the Solway, the lonely country at the back of Skiddaw, the Ullswater fells and some of the mountains around Wasdale, the High Street range, the wide expanse of the Eden valley and, behind it, the Northern Pennines – an unusual, if not superb, view. One of its more interesting features, I think, is the sight of Bowscale Fell, just across the Caldew, with the tip of Bowscale Tarn, just visible behind a fold in the fellside. The tarn, rather like Blind Tarn in the Coniston fells, hangs in a little saucer not far below the summit. If the rims of the saucers are ever broken or washed away both tarns will spill into the valley. On my last visit to Carrock there was no sound not even the chatter of scree or the trickle of water, and it was difficult to realize that men had known these lonely slopes for 2,000 years or more.

GLARAMARA
July 1963

I have never thought of Glaramara, at 2,560 feet, as a mountain, still less as a peak. To me it has always been a fell, a long, straggling line of fell with not much mountain shape and hardly any beginning or end. It is not very obvious where it all starts and there are so many summits and bumps along the ridge that it is not always clear whether or not one has arrived on the top and, sometimes, whether one is going up or down. People rarely talk of going 'up' Glaramara. More often they are going 'over' or 'along' the fell. This is not to suggest that Glaramara is anything but a most splendid section of upland Lakeland. For me, it is a fell with one of the loveliest names in the district, full of interest with surprises around every corner, a magnificent viewpoint, and a place of great charm and individuality. The little tarns scattered along its undulating summit ridge are among the finest in the National Park.

Like so many other fells of character Glaramara has no clearly recognizable shape, although it is an isolated mass occupying almost the whole of the area between Grains Gill and Langstrath Beck. It rarely obtrudes on the skyline, and often its switchback ridge seems to melt almost shyly into other more impressive and adjoining contours. Many people identifying Lakeland peaks from a distant point might fail completely to pick out the fell at all, or, having sorted out the others declare, "So that lump over there must be Glaramara."

Fortunately for those of us who prefer our mountains to be quiet and lonely, Glaramara is not a popular fell. It was almost trackless until a holiday guest house was established near the Seatoller road end some years ago, and borrowed 'Glaramara' as its name. Since then the fell has been much more in use. There is now a pleasant path along the ridge, and other tracks wend upwards from the valley. Glaramara is still less soiled by mass tourism, litter, cairns and other signs of over popularity than many less worthy places. One reason for this comparative neglect might be that Glaramara has come to be regarded as a nasty place in mist or bad weather, an impression worth encouraging. It is easy in difficult conditions to get lost on Glaramara and even with a compass and the ability to use it particular care is sometimes required. The hummocky nature of the ground, the crags on either side of the ridge, some bad stretches of bog, and the deeply cut gills can make the steering of a compass course a tricky problem. I remember once going across the fell from the remote little pool of Tarn at Leaves to Stockley Bridge in very bad weather. Although I know the place fairly well it was necessary in more than one place to retrace my steps and work out a better route. The fell must be one of the best places in the district for trying out young people in the use of map and compass.

Glaramara was probably the original name for the rocky summit of the fell but it has come to be applied to the whole ridge from Thornythwaite to Allen Crags, including Thornythwaite Fell itself, while Rosthwaite Fell might also be included in the massif by the less finicky visitor. In effect, Glaramara is almost the northeastern spur of the Scafells since there is only a shallow drop at the end of the long ridge to the summit of Esk Hause at nearly 2,500 feet before the steep surge up to Great End. But the character of Glaramara, well-wooded on its lower slopes and rounded, tumbled and sprawling in its upper reaches, has little in common with the Scafells. There is no pleasanter way to the highest land in England than along the Glaramara switchback but when you look across the Hause from the top of Allen Crags you are looking at a different, wilder country.

Perhaps Glaramara's most prominent feature is the wonderful hanging valley of Combe Gill – Combe Ghyll to some people – which faces northwards up the length of Borrowdale but is surprisingly little visited by tourists, although well known to climbers. The valley contains many rock routes, notably on Raven Crag which faces east and is split by the fine gully which first attracted climbers into the Combe about seventy years ago. Facing this crag is the remarkable mass of rock known as Doves' Nest caves. There is no place quite like this in the Lake District. A great buttress of rock has slipped down the fellside but instead of crashing into scree at the foot of the cliff its fall has been arrested and it now leans back against the parent crag, leaving great fissures and caves underneath and at the back. These are the caves and you will need candles or headlamps together with the necessary climbing skill to explore them. The game is a mixture of pot-holing and climbing with some rewarding, quite exciting routes. Some of the climbs, after you have emerged from the depths, continue on the outside walls above. You can be dry and warm in the darkness one minute, and cold and wet in the upper air a few moments later.

Glaramara is more often reached from Combe Gill than from other directions, apart perhaps from the ridge route from Allen Crags, but for the climber there is an interesting approach from Langstrath by way of Cam Crag Ridge, which is about 700 feet high and leads to the top of Rosthwaite Fell and thence to Glaramara. It is a very easy route for the climber, but not for the walker. I only mention it here because the ridge is, in effect, the ascent of a mountainside where the hands are required as well as the feet – a circumstance fairly unusual in Lakeland.

One of the principal glories of Glaramara is the walk to Allen Crags along the broad grassy ridge, with the wonderful succession of lovely tarns and the magnificent views over most of Lakeland which are continually provided. Only one tarn, High House Tarn, is named by the one-inch Ordnance Survey map but there must be at least six of them between the summit and Allen Crags and almost all of them are gems. If one approaches the ridge from Combe Gill there are one or two small tarns near the col but the finest collection is beyond Pinnacle Bield, the largest of then being High House Tarn. There are trout in this delightful tarn which may be used as the foreground for a photographic picture of Pike o' Stickle, 2 or 3 miles away to the southeast. A few hundred yards away to the south lies Lincomb Tarn which is a real jewel.

All the way along this ridge the views are magnificent, for Glaramara is not overshadowed by any other mountain. The walk southwards towards the highest land in England is probably the special glory of the fell. The best view of all is possibly that from the summit northwards along the curve of Borrowdale with the wooded valley in the middle distance and then, beyond, Derwentwater and its islands.

Glaramara will always be a favourite fell of mine for it is a place quite unlike anywhere else in Lakeland, full of quiet beauty and individuality and with plenty of scope for mild adventuring. A shy fell, perhaps, but although not particularly photogenic from a distance it can be one of the most rewarding places in Lakeland to visit with a colour camera.

THE INCOMPARABLE SCREES
March 1964

The most dramatic mountain view in England for the motorist is not the sight of the Scafells or Helvellyn, nor the ridges of Blencathra nor the crags of Great Gable, nor even the rock turrets of the Langdale Pikes. No, the most breathtaking mountain picture in Lakeland to be seen from the roadway is probably the northwest front of Whin Rigg and the western slopes of Illgill Head. These are strangely unfamiliar, mountain names to some of you, perhaps. They're only small mountains – not much more than half the height of Scafell Pike – but your first view of them as you drive through the woods near Wasdale Hall towards the grandest dale head in England, if you have picked the right day, can pull you up in yards. We call them, more familiarly, the Wastwater Screes or, as often as not, just 'The Screes'.

They rise perhaps 1,500 feet within the space of less than half a mile from the farther shore of England's deepest lake – vast tilted rivers of scree poised steeply above the lake and capped by wild crags savagely split by dark, vertical ravines. Seen through the trees at the seaward end of the lake, especially in autumn or winter, the colours are really exciting – the russet tints of the dead bracken, the red streaks of iron ore in the crags and screes, the rich dark umber of the precipices, and the green, brown and purple splashes of the hanging gardens caught among the rocks. The picture is always changing, according to the lighting and the time of year. Below, Wastwater may be dark and brooding, storm-tossed and flecked white with driven spray, or sparkling in the sunlight, and the lake's moods will be echoed on the mountain wall. But no matter the weather the overall effect is always dramatic and inspiring, and sometimes even awesome. Here, among fantastic minarets of rock and the black cavernous gullies, could be the abode of trolls.

Nowhere else in Lakeland can such a splendid chaos of rock and scree – nearly 2 miles of it – be seen from the roadway; nowhere else in England is there such an exciting 'surprise view' as this. See this mountain wall lit by the evening sun, or towards the end of a short winter's afternoon, with the rain stopped and the rocks glistening, or perhaps some patches of snow hanging in the gullies, and you have caught a view that can stand comparison – in dramatic quality – with many of the much vaunted continental mountain scenes.

I must not give the impression that the screes are only to be enjoyed by the motorist. The rewards for the walker and climber are far, far greater. You may walk along The Screes themselves and under the crags, or along the ridge on top of the precipices. You may climb the crags by one of the gullies, or walk up to the top ridge from either end of the lake, or even from Burnmoor, or from lonely Miterdale. You may, merely study the line of cliffs from the opposite side of the lake. Over the years I've managed to do all these things, some of them many times, so that now I feel justified in suggesting that, for their height, these must be the most satisfying 'little hills' in Lakeland. Undoubtedly one of their most rewarding features is the walk along the length of the ridge – a simple airy expedition providing magnificent views of Wasdale Head and the central mountains of Lakeland in one direction, and the sea and the pile stacks of Windscale in the other. The real thrill of the walk is the wonderful view of the whole length of Wastwater, seemingly almost vertically below, the toy houses and farms at Strands and Nether Wasdale, and, best of all, the peeps down the gullies, and down into the crazy, rock scenery. For some of it does look rather crazy – huge crumbling pillars poised fantastically above the lake and ready to fall, although I've no doubt they've looked just like this for thousands of years.

When you look at The Screes from below, the ridge looks long and almost level but in fact there are two summits. The higher is Illgill Head, nearly 2,000 feet above sea level, which rises about halfway along Wastwater. The other, the right-hand summit as seen from the lake shore, is Whin Rigg, more than 200 feet lower, and just opposite Wasdale Hall at the western end of the lake. Between the two summits lies The Screes, the name loosely given to the whole ridge which should really only be applied to the steep portion of crag and fellside dropping steeply to the lake. To some people the scree slopes may look almost perpendicular, although I believe they are no steeper than 45 degrees, but the crags above are certainly steep enough to soar to the vertical in places.

They say that the scree continues at the same steepness down to the bottom of the lake – you can check this on the six-inch Ordnance Survey map – and the lake sinks to a depth of 258 feet, the deepest inland gulf in the country. The bottom, immediately beneath Illgill Head, touches well below sea level.

Up on the ridge, halfway between the two summits is a small peaty tarn, with a smaller one beside it, and eastwards the slope falls away easily into the little visited valley of Miterdale and down by the Whillan Beck to the valley of the Esk. Of the two summit views, that from Illgill Head is possibly the finer, with its rather more intimate panorama of the Wasdale hills, but the more dramatic view is the Whin Rigg picture of the shattered profile of The Screes plunging down into the dark depths of Wastwater.

Several times I have been to The Screes to climb. Of the two main gullies falling down from Whin Rigg towards the lake, the one on the left, as seen from Wasdale Hall, is the longer and is called Great Gully, while the one a little further to the right is C Gully. Both provide magnificent severe rock climbs and each time I have been there, no matter what the weather, the pitches have been wet, sometimes with waterfalls pouring down them. The last time I was in Great Gully we had just emerged, wet through and rather dirty, from the top pitch and were coiling the rope when a fox got up almost beneath our feet and ran streaking through the heather and the bracken down towards the Irt.

Great Gully has 17 pitches and the remains of an aeroplane are embedded among the rocks below the first one. Both climbs are among the most rewarding of their type in Lakeland. The rock scenery is strikingly dramatic, with fine amphitheatres as you progress up the crag, but the crumbling, iron-spattered rock on the vegetation covered walls has so far discouraged much exploration outside the gullies, although one or two routes have been pioneered in recent years. But the crags are certainly among the least explored among the bigger precipices of Lakeland and there still remain big areas of probably treacherous rock where no man has ever been.

Most Lake District visitors, however, don't climb rocks and an easier expedition for the average person might be the traverse of the lakeside path which runs underneath the crags and along The Screes. This trip has been variously described as 'impossible' or 'very easy'. For the average performer it is a perfectly feasible ramble although at one point it is rather rough and becomes a bit of a scramble. Early guidebooks described this as a very dangerous expedition, claiming that one risked being struck by boulders trundling down the scree slopes but this is, of course, nonsense. You must be careful at one place but it can be managed, if necessary, on a wild, wet night with a poorish torch, as two of us once discovered.

One interesting feature of The Screes is the big slice carved out of the fellside about half a mile to the west of the summit of Whin Rigg – Greathall Gill. It is rather like a long crater running down from the ridge and is quite unlike anywhere else in the district. The gill seems to have been formed by the crumbling of a band of granite leaving curious rock fingers, pink scree and strange banks of sand. In between are stretches of grass, bubbling streams, pleasant ledges and sheep trods, making the ravine a rather strange, other worldly sort of place. Iron used to be worked there at one time, I believe.

My last visit to The Screes was to one of the gullies which we found even wetter and greasier than usual. Holds were masked with bright green moss and slime, water sprayed off the gully walls and we clawed our way up cool, dank chimneys in musky gloom. But outside, framed by the black streaming walls, we could see the lake far below and a segment of rather unfamiliar sunlit countryside.

It's a different country around The Screes and it is still, fortunately, not so well known. Years ago I used to think that The Screes were only really worth visiting when the day was too wet and miserable for anything more worthwhile – a trudge around the lake and over the ridge in the rain, just for the exercise. But with advancing years and much less energy I think it's a place to visit for its own sake – a place where you can get right away from the summer crowds and see sights and views quite different from those in any other part of Lakeland.

HELM CRAG
May 1964

Perhaps we shouldn't call Helm Crag – hardly 1,300 feet high – a mountain, but as it must be one of the best known hills in the country we can't very well ignore it. It has more character and shape than many mountains twice its height and a graceful charm that, for me, seems to typify the peaceful loveliness of a Lakeland summer evening. Unfortunately, however, many people know Helm Crag only as the hill on the right as they travel down from Dunmail Raise from Keswick. It means only 'The Lion and The Lamb', one of the popular tourist sights of Lakeland. For 200 years or more travellers going over the pass on horseback or in waggonette or motor coach have looked across at the shapely fell, made sure they could pick out The Lion and The Lamb, and then carried on their way, well satisfied. Few have known the name of the fell and perhaps fewer still have cared. All that mattered was that they should have the eyesight and the imagination to spot what tens of thousands of others had seen before them. What percentage of all those thousands have bothered to scramble up the little hill and see the rocks from close at hand I can't guess, but for a summit only half a mile away from the main highway through Lakeland, Helm Crag is comparatively neglected.

It seems a pity that a grand little fell like Helm Crag should be saddled to its fancied resemblance to animals and other objects and regarded by the uninformed as little more than a peep show. For, with the necessary imagination, you can spot many odd things on top. From somewhere near the summit of Dunmail Raise the summit rocks are said to resemble a huge cannon or howitzer, and from lower down the pass they become an old woman seated at an organ. You are not necessarily looking at the same rocks in seeing the different figures and the issue is further confused by there being two sets of The Lion and The Lamb, as well as a Lion Couchant. I have never bothered to sort it all out but Mr Wainwright, the guidebook writer, says the 'official' Lion and Lamb are formed by the rocks at the southeast end of the summit ridge and are correctly viewed from the Swan Hotel. At the northwest end of the ridge are the rocks forming the crouching lion (popularly 'The Lion and The Lamb') as seen from halfway up the pass, or 'The Howitzer' as seen from Dunmail Raise. These also provide 'The Old Lady at the Organ'.

The summit of Helm Crag is a much more interesting place than all this roadside fancy might lead one to expect. It is, for example, one of the very few summits in the Lake District only attainable by the use of hands as well as feet. The actual summit is the top of the head of the (unofficial) Lion or Howitzer, although the Ordnance Survey use the head of the official Lion, which is slightly lower. You scramble to the top of Helm Crag up a sloping slab to reach an airy perch above a wilderness of tumbled rock.

There is more rock and crag on top of modest little Helm Crag than on the summits of many of the bigger mountains of Lakeland. The summit ridge itself carries the strangely shaped rocks you see from the road but there are also many other lumps of crag besides a moat-like depression and a rocky parapet high above the precipice of Raven Crag. Flowers grow in the rocky clefts and in the shattered remains of what must once have been an impressive crag are many caves. Somewhere within this magnificent chaos of tumbled rocks that litters the curious trough just below the summit there is, I believe a particularly fine inner cave where you could hide a company, but when ever I have gone exploring up there I've always found myself without a torch. And nearly always with my dog Sambo who will keep disappearing into awkward places, and constantly requiring rescue. Some time I'll remember to take a torch and perhaps leave Sambo behind for once.

The last time I was on Helm Crag was a sunny Sunday last winter and I remember sitting up there thinking how fortunate I was to be perched in such a delightful spot on such a perfect morning. There seemed to be nobody else on the hill and Sambo had gone off exploring on his own so that the peace and quietude was complete. The mists were still hanging in the meadows but above them the fells soared steeply towards the blue skies. A cotton wool haze lay over the waters of Windermere and the woodlands spiked through the greyness, but the fellside sparkled in the sunlight and here and there a tarn or a mountain pool flashed silvery as a mirror. Perched on the head of 'The Lion' I could see and hear the cars going over Dunmail Raise, 500 feet below – little toy cars in blue, yellow or grey, they seemed – and the pleasant sounds of pails rattling in a dairy or farm dogs at play came whinging up the fellside on this stillest of winter mornings.

On the way up the fell I had disturbed the jackdaws in the little crag where the holly trees grow and for half an hour I listened to the liquid call of a curlew mournfully circling the summit without spotting him. Sometimes I could just catch the murmur of a waterfall in the next valley but there was little else to hear and the fell country seemed deep in its winter sleep.

Helm Crag is the perfect setting for a warm summer evening. From the summit there is often a wonderful sunset view and the vale of Easedale below is one of the most perfect places in Lakeland to reach at the end of a long day. There is a peaceful serenity about this little valley that has always captivated me, besides attracting many people of discernment to make their homes there.

You can walk up Helm Crag in half an hour or so and continue easily along the ridge to Gibson Knott and Calf Crag, returning by way of Far Easedale – one of the most rewarding evening or half-day walks in the district. Or you can finish an Easedale walk by coming down the front of Helm Crag as the blue shadows slowly creep up the golden hillsides and the smoke rises quietly from the cottage windows. Soon the first lights will be appearing through the dusk in Grasmere and another simple day in the hills comes to an end.

When the time comes that I have to give up rock climbing and serious fell walking – I hope it's a long time off yet – I like to think that I will still be able to get up Helm Crag and enjoy the quiet scenery, and perhaps watch the sunset over the Langdales.

GRASMOOR
August 1964

You can see Grasmoor from heights all over Lakeland. It is a lordly, sprawling hump at the end of a hummocky ridge. From close at hand the mountain looks even better than it is. Grasmoor may not come within my ten favourite mountains but I'm bound to admit that the view of its western flank from some places in Buttermere is one of the most impressive sights of bulk and steepness to be seen from any Lakeland main road. Some may agree that Grasmoor, with its acres of smoothly sloping turf, can be a dull mountain in places but, using your imagination a little and choosing the right day, you could compare its great wall of broken crags towering over Crummock Water with the way the North Wall of the Eiger dominates Lauterbrunnen and the Grindelwald valley. Please don't misunderstand me. The Eiger is three times as high, nearly twice as steep, and an exceptionally formidable ascent compared with the rather boring scramble up the crumbling rock of Grasmoor End, but there is a certain similarity if you care to seek it out – especially under intimidating weather conditions. Seen from Lanthwaite Green the dark wall completely dwarfs the farms at its foot, and manmade things take on humble proportions against the towering rock and scree.

Not far from the foot of the wall the picnickers and campers stake their claim in summertime and sometimes perhaps these visitors, comfortably settled in near Cinderdale Beck, look up with apprehension at the rocky face and wonder whether they are really safe from falling chunks of it. There is really no danger, for any loose rock coming away after the winter ice would come to rest on the screes long before reaching the meadows. There is little fear of climbers dislodging pieces of rock, for they don't bother to go there. Grasmoor End looks impressive but the face only yields two gully climbs of moderate difficulty which are hardly worth bothering with when there are so many much better things to climb a mile or two further up the valley.

There is another fine looking crag, on the mountain – and that is the cirque of Dove Crags which drop away to the north from the summit. Here the rock is far from sound. Although one or two of the gullies have been climbed the place is normally avoided by climbers nowadays.

Grasmoor is a walkers' mountain, one of the easiest in the district to ascend if you go up from round 'the back' or along the ridge. It is a remarkably fine viewpoint, and it can also provide an interesting day for the botanist. Apart from its craggy western end and the northern circle of Dove Crags, this is a much grassier mountain than most others in Lakeland, besides being exceptionally well-clothed with flowers and shrubs. I have been told by one authority that the mountain probably grows more flora than any other in the district, and I can certainly speak of the lushness of its turf, the variety of its mountain flowers and the delicious abundance of its bilberries. In season, you can walk across the mountain and feel you are strolling through a mile long rock garden. I dare say, if you tried hard enough, you could find forty or fifty plants in just one corner. Almost anything, it seems, can grow on Grasmoor, but not the red alpine catchfly, Lakeland's rarest plant. To find this you have to scramble across Gasgale Beck and scramble up the steep front of Hobcarton Crag more than a mile away.

I suppose one reason for the plenitude of its flora is the Skiddaw slate of which Grasmoor and many of the surrounding fells are made. This ancient rock breaks up into friable scree and brings about the gently swelling shapes of these northwest mountain slopes. The southern face of the long ridge that starts at Causey Pike and finishes on Grasmoor has a reddish tinge quite different from most other Lakeland fells, and the switchback nature of this range seems completely characteristic and completely satisfying to study from across the valley. Mostly, I like to see Grasmoor in the evening when the westering sun glows on the reddish screes and you can pick out the heather and the juniper among the crags.

You can run down off Grasmoor into Buttermere on some of the most perfect scree in the district and this can be the rewarding end of a good day exploring the mountain. Apart from the plant life the principal feature of the summit plateau is the splendid view and the Dove Crags escarpment. Here is a grassy basin encircled by steep crags, and the combe looks as if it ought to contain a tarn. There is no sign of there ever having been one here and there is no tarn that I can remember on the mountain. A few pleasant waterfalls exist in Cinderdale Beck but there are no pools – only the long length of Crummock Water washing the mountain's western skirts.

From the summit you see the receding ridges of High Stile and Red Pike, Great Gable, Kirk Fell and Pillar, and the Scafells, and the Irish Sea and the Solway Firth are often clearly visible. I can't remember whether the Isle of Man can be seen on the right day or whether the Loweswater or the Buttermere fells are in the way, but most of northern Lakeland from St Bees Head to Helvellyn and northwards to Skiddaw is on view. Only southern Lakeland is hidden.

Buttermere is one of the least spoiled of the principal valleys of Lakeland and 200 years ago Father Thomas West selected Lanthwaite Hill as one of the most important viewpoints, or 'stations' as he called them, in the district. He rode up Buttermere, taking notes as he went, for what was to become the first real guide to Lakeland, and most people would agree with this choice, if not with some of his other preferences. Approaching Buttermere from the north you see the mountains gradually unfolding as you move up the dale, and there is the striking view of Grasmoor End rising from the meadows. This is Lakeland scenery at its very best, and the road under Grasmoor and Rannerdale Knotts must be one of the finest bits of unfenced motor road in the district. Too popular, perhaps, in summertime nowadays with cars parked along every yard of it, but out of season there is no lovelier place to stop and eat your sandwiches and enjoy the quietude and the mountain panorama all around.

Grasmoor is the undoubted king of this area – perhaps the fourteenth highest mountain in Lakeland, but the biggest in the northwestern fells. There may be few mountains in Europe older than Grasmoor and his neighbours and he will always remain a principal Buttermere attraction – a burly, red-faced giant lording it over the lesser heights and guarding, with Mellbreak across the water, the entrance to Nicholas Size's 'Secret Valley'.

YEWBARROW
October 1965

My first acquaintance with Yewbarrow must have been about thirty-five years ago when we used to run down the screes of Dore Head at the northern end of the peak as a suitably flourishing ending to a day's climbing on Pillar Rock. We thought this the finest scree run in the Lake District. Perhaps it was, but it is now useless as a means of quick descent. All the stones have been rolled and washed away. Perhaps Great Hell Gate will go the same way in time.

Since then I've been on the mountain many times but it was only on my last visit, earlier this year, that I realized how steep Yewbarrow is – on all sides. Perhaps I'm getting old, but I can't think of any other mountain as small as this one and yet so steep all around. Undoubtedly, for all its modest height – little more than 2,000 feet – Yewbarrow is a real mountain, with much more than its fair share of crag, a fine cock's comb of a ridge and some of the most exciting summit views in Lakeland. From its craggy top you can look down into perhaps the finest dale head in the district or across at the cliffs of Scafell, or turn around and peer down into the depths of Wastwater. This last is one of the great attractions of Yewbarrow – the sight of the dark lake below your feet and, in the distance, the sea, so that you might be high up in the Cuillins looking across Hebridean waters.

Little Yewbarrow has much of the character of a Cuillin peak, for its long, narrow summit is ringed with crag on both sides, cleft here and there by dark gullies. Each end of the ridge is protected by cliff. The traverse of the mountain, if you keep on the ridge all the way, is more of a climb than a scramble and beyond the compass of ordinary walkers. Not many Lakeland summits are protected in this way.

My last visit was on a Bank Holiday, a time when I usually keep well away from Lakeland, preferring solitude to crowds. This day we had seen little traffic along the

Cumberland coast and I had been tempted to drive into Wasdale. Having got so far it seemed almost sacrilege to be motoring in such surroundings, so I stopped the car and strolled up Yewbarrow to stretch my legs and savour the heights. It must have been four or five years since I had last been up Yewbarrow and I had forgotten it is such a rocky place. I kept straight up the ridge of Bell Rib and when I reached the crag I was glad I had left my dog Sambo at the bottom with the family. He is well accustomed to steep places but not so steep as this. Perhaps this is no place for a solitary climber, but I had been there before and worked my way up the final wall and chimneys with considerable care.

As I went higher there were fascinating peeps across to Burnmoor Tarn and, to the left, the lonely pool of Low Tarn underneath Red Pike, and when I finally reached the top there was Gable to the right and Pillar straight ahead, and the fields of Wasdale Head far below and deeply carved valleys all around. This ridge is almost the perfect grandstand, with the finest mountains in England – Pillar, Gable and the Scafells – in a ring all around you and the heart of mountain Lakeland 2,000 feet below you.

A stiff breeze was sending the cloud shadows racing across the sunlit slopes but the picture was not quite the same as I remembered it long ago. For the head of Wasdale, just beyond the lake, was a gaily-coloured patchwork of tents – blue, yellow, red, all the colours of the rainbow – and some of the mystery of the secret valley of our youth seemed to have disappeared. What a pity, I thought, they hadn't sited this camping ground in the woods at the other end of the lake, and left the dale head unspoiled.

Yewbarrow rightly takes its place among the Wasdale giants. Its wedge shape is prominent in the foreground as you drive northeastwards up the dale and it is a real guardian of the shrine of Wasdale Head. You drive around its skirts as you approach the sanctuary and the hotel is perched at its foot. The broom on the craggy bluffs of the fell makes a brave show and the waters of the lake lap its feet.

Mosedale Beck and Over Beck almost ring the mountain on other sides so that the fell stands alone with the scramble of Stirrup Crag above Dore Head separating it from its nearest neighbour, Red Pike. The little valley of Over Beck above Bowderdale Farm is one of the gems of Lakeland and overhanging the valley is the cliff of Overbeck Crag or Dropping Crag, nowadays crisscrossed with climbing routes. This is a good place to take beginners. It is a better practice ground than the upper cliffs of Bell Rib. From the crag you can run down the band to Bowderdale in a few minutes.

On my last visit I met a disconsolate couple on the way down who asked me how one got up the mountain. They had tried what seemed to them the straightforward way over Bell Rib but had been turned back by the crags and couldn't see another way. I suggested the tourist route beyond Overbeck Crag and they said they would try it as they wanted to look down on Wasdale and across to Pillar. I thought it was rather wonderful that here was a little mountain, right in the very heart of things, but without a really easy way up and by no means over-scratched with tracks.

WHO WAS ST SUNDAY?
January 1966

Somewhere in an old guidebook, published more than fifty years ago, I remember reading, 'St Sunday Crag is the Ullswater mountain'. It is not a bad description when you come to think about it, for St Sunday Crag dominates the western reach of Ullswater far more dramatically than Helvellyn and, in a sense, commands the whole length of the lake better than any other mountain. Yet its summit is disappointing and the mountain is not especially popular. Not many people bother with the ascent for its own sake, but are more likely to use the mountain as a pleasant route off Fairfield. It is very strange for St Sunday Crag is a massive, soaring fell, one of the steepest in Lakeland, with a fine shape when seen from any angle.

Who St Sunday was I have no idea. W.G. Collingwood suggested the name might be derived from St Sanctan, but this does not help a great deal. There is a St Sunday's Beck to the southeast of Kendal, but no apparent connection between the two. Perhaps, though, the name does not matter very much. It trips readily enough off the tongue, although it is really surprising how few people know the mountain.

I was last there in October, climbing some of the new routes on the crag. When I happened to mention this a few days later to a friend who has been walking the fells for years he confessed he had never been on the mountain and had never even noticed the crag. Yet the Grisedale face of the mountain which drops nearly 2,000 feet in half a mile is one of the most dramatic fellsides in the district and the crags, below the summit ridge, are nearly a mile long. My friend is by no means alone in not knowing about this long line of crag, as big as several Napes Ridges crowded together, for rock climbers had missed it for fifty years and only started making climbs there about ten years ago.

Seen from the valley the crags look relatively insignificant because of the length and steepness of the fellside below them. It is only when you get among them that you realise what you have been missing. The crag is not among the best in Lakeland, but at least there is a lot of it, the rock is good, and some of the climbs, particularly on the Great Nose and the Pillar, are quite impressive. So far about twenty routes have been made and there is scope for more new climbing there, although the approaches to the crag – for the climber – can be rather long and tedious.

There is much more to St Sunday Crag than this rather restricted appeal for the rock climber. The mountain is not only a shapely, impressive fell but a magnificent viewpoint. The summit itself, as I have indicated, is rather dull, but from a point a little way down towards the north and, indeed, from almost any point along this northeast ridge there are wonderful views of Ullswater – perhaps the best views of the lake you can get from any of the surrounding fells. The descent from the summit down this long ridge, across the shoulder of Birks, and through the steeply wooded slopes of Glenamara Park, is among the particular joys of a visit to Patterdale. This is a track for walking down rather than up, for the view below you all the way – the lake curving around the side of Place Fell, with its tiny islands riding like yachts at anchor, and the scene slowly changing from crag and woodland to the quiet pastoral beauty of the eastern end.

The hard way up St Sunday Crag is to plough up the rather dreary zigzags from Elmhow in Grisedale, and this is the way the climber goes, but there is quite an interesting route from Deepdale by way of the east ridge, or better still, the mountain can be approached from Fairfield. I suppose I must have come off Fairfield this way dozens of times – over Cofa Pike, down to Deepdale Hause and then, pleasantly and easily, over the top of St Sunday Crag and on to Patterdale for food and drink. Alternatively the walker can get his peak the long, easy way by walking up Grisedale to the tarn, and then working his way up the screes to Deepdale Hause and on to the summit, with the run down to Patterdale as dessert.

Before the rock climbers found the crag, the Grisedale face of the mountain used to be an interesting place for wild flowers, perhaps because hardly anybody ever went there. I hope and believe it will continue so, for the climbs are not likely to attract crowds of Great Gable proportions, and you can still have them to yourself and watch the processions moving over Striding Edge across the valley. Perhaps we have been on the crags half a dozen times, but we have never seen anybody else there.

Although the summit of St Sunday Crag is not an especially interesting place and only a moderate viewpoint the neighbouring top of Gavel Pike, across a little saddle, is a pleasant, airy peak and well worth a visit. One rewarding view from the main summit – perhaps its main feature – is the splendid peep into the coves below the summit of Helvellyn, but the bulk of this mountain, and of Fairfield, too, prevents many distant views. The sweeps down into Grisedale and Deepdale, however, maintain St Sunday Crag's dominance and the views to the northeast, once the descent is begun, will always justify the climb to the top.

CAUSEY PIKE
March 1966

The shapely white cone seen in the background of many of the Lakeland winter scenes pictured by the early Keswick photographers is Causey Pike, a distinctive little fell that presides gracefully over the Vale of Newlands. They chose it, presumably – as often as not with the still waters of Derwentwater in the foreground – because, from the right angle, it has the sort of shape we associate with mountains; pyramidal and getting steeper towards the top. And also, perhaps, because it holds the snow so smoothly on its steeply sloping sides.

But Causey Pike, it could be argued, is not really much of a mountain, being merely the first incident on an extremely pleasant ridge, and not even granted the favour of a height on the one-inch map of the Ordnance Survey. It does top the 2,000 contour by a few feet – although there's no agreement on exactly how many – but the scant references to the fell in the guidebooks are largely confined to remarks that Causey Pike is a pleasant way off the ridge. Perhaps this little fell, with no hidden mysteries to explore and no real crags or tumbling gills or tarns, is not a very important mountain, but at least it has a personality of its own. Its heather-decked summit is one of the happiest retreats I can imagine on a sunny spring day, with not too many folk about.

The most important thing about Causey Pike is its shape and especially the top few hundred feet. There are not many Lake District mountains that carry almost a label on their summits so that you can recognize them from any angle. Bowfell may be one and Pike o' Stickle another. Causey Pike must certainly be included. Baddeley calls it 'Napoleon's Face' but doesn't bother to say or explain why and, fifty years later, Heaton Cooper delightfully describes the peak as shaped like the bent horn of an old sheep. Occasionally, in wintertime, Causey Pike has looked to me rather like the sagging corner of a badly erected ridge tent, which is far from poetic, with Sail, further along the ridge, appearing exactly like its name – a ship's canvas billowing out in the wind.

This best known view of Causey Pike is not its only identifying feature. When the fell is seen sideways on the summit appears as a line of wrinkles – a miniature Crinkle Crags, or, as somebody has written, rather like the humps of a sea serpent. From almost every angle – and Causey Pike seems to have the facility of popping up between all manner of greater and lesser heights – the summit is unmistakable, in just the same way as the rocky pinnacles like Bidein Druim nan Ramh on the Skye Ridge, although lower than its neighbours, can always be recognized at a glance.

The last time I walked over the top was on a pleasant sunny afternoon when two of us circled the fells that encircle the Coledale Beck, taking in Sail, Eel Crag, Hobcarton and Grisedale Pike and then threading the leafy lanes back to Stair through the evening shadows. I remember the heather couches on the top of Causey Pike and the lovely, restful view of the surrounding fells, basking in the sunshine, and the warm greens and browns in the winding dales below our feet. When we had dozed and smoked we continued on our way along the beautifully soaring ridge towards Wandope with the valley of Rigg Beck down on our left climbing up to the little col that looks down to Crummock and Buttermere.

Several times in recent years I've been on the lower slopes of Causey Pike, or down in the lane by Stair, waiting for one or other of the men trying to set up a new twenty-four-hours fell record. More than once Causey Pike has been the last peak of all in a very long day embracing between fifty and sixty tops and we have waited anxiously, watches in hand, for the runner and his companions to appear on the summit. All at once, we have spotted the figure, no bigger than a matchstick on the top and then another and another. Within a few minutes, they have been down in the lane and pressing on determinedly, with only a few road miles to the finish at Keswick. Once it was dark when they came over the top, and we first saw their torches, the lights pricking the black shape of the mountain as they edged their way down the summit rocks towards the easy run down from Sleet Hause.

Holiday time attracts the visitors to Causey Pike as it is such a straightforward easy walk from Keswick and the views of Derwentwater and the fells are fine from the top. If you want the fell to yourself you should go up mid-week or out of season.

Causey Pike is a typical fell of the 'slate' country, steep-sided, smoothly contoured and grassy, but breaking away into little crags here and there. Perhaps there is no finer mountain viewpoint in the Keswick area, no other height so easily attained with so much lake and dale in the foreground and so much mountain spread all around. I always think affectionately of Causey Pike – one of the shapeliest grandstands in the district.

LIFE BEFORE THE DELUGE
April 2001

How clearly I remember 1951 – the year when the Lake District National Park was formed, and the magazine *Cumbria* started life in Clapham and I began my fortnightly contributions to the Country Diary in *The Guardian*. All three have now lasted for half a century and, although my *Guardian* pieces won't go on forever, the other two show no sign of weakening. I well remember attending the very first meeting of the Lake District Planning Board in Kendal in September of that year – and many subsequent meetings – and, for some years, I was a co-opted member of one of the Board's main committees. But my interest in the National Park had been stimulated many years before for I knew most of the main campaigners quite well. These included Sir Norman Birkett (later Lord Birkett, who wrote the foreword to my first book, *Inside the Real Lakeland*, in 1960), the Rev H. H. Symonds who had founded the Friends of the Lake District in 1936, and Professor R.S.T. Chorley (later the first Lord Chorley) with whom I had regularly climbed on Dow Crag and Gimmer Crag whenever he came up from London to preside at Westmorland Quarter Sessions. Without these three men, and a few others, there would have been no Lake District National Park today.

Strangely, I had also been involved with *Cumbria* magazine from its very earliest days for I was a close friend of its very first editor, Leslie Hewkin, before it was taken over by Harry Scott of the Dalesman Publishing Company at Clapham. Leslie, prominently associated with the Youth Hostels Association, was an early member of the Lake District Planning Board. In the early days he got me to write the occasional article for his little magazine, *Cumbria* – probably the first time this name had been generally applied to the Lake District. Then, when Harry Scott took over the magazine, I regularly, for a few years, contributed a monthly series of articles, 'Portraits of Mountains', dealing with a different Lake District mountain each month.

So my association with both these admirable institutions, the Lake District National Park and *Cumbria* magazine, both now celebrating their jubilee, has been a long and happy one.

The Lake District, of course, was a very different place fifty years ago – far quieter, with not a quarter of the traffic of today. The old constituent counties, Cumberland, Westmorland and Lancashire, were still in existence – and remained so for another twenty-three years – so that, driving north, you left Westmorland and dropped down into Cumberland at the top of Dunmail Raise. (Westmorland folk always used to say: "Nowt good ever came ower t'Raise"). This was years before the straightening out, widening and 'upgrading' of the main road into Lakeland to facilitate the passage of the mass tourism that the new road invited. The A591 was then a narrow, twisting road, without modern kerbs and with not many filling stations, and since there was no overall Cumbria road authority the roads over Wrynose and Hardknott passes came under the jurisdiction of the three county councils, which resulted in startlingly different road surfaces. Part of the Westmorland section, for instance, was concreted, while there was tarmacadam or loose chippings on the others.

During the Second World War the passes had been used for the training of Bren gun-carrier drivers and became little better than a muddy river bed, deeply rutted, littered with boulders and streaming with water. I remember driving over the passes in 1947, before they were repaired, when their passage was something of an adventure. All this, of course, was many, many years before the motorway and the Kendal bypass, both of which, we were told, would relieve the traffic congestion in Kendal. But neither had much, if any, effect, the situation now being worse than it's ever been.

The tracks on the fells fifty years ago bore little resemblance to the wide, ugly, stony excrescences that pass for paths nowadays. In the early 1950s the fell paths were, mostly, narrow grass tracks, not greatly different from the paths I remember from my early climbing days in the 1920s. And there weren't nearly so many of them. For example, there was no track going over Glaramara and, before the war and up to at least the 1950s, two of us often used to go to this trackless mountain, in bad weather, specifically to improve our compass work. With its steep transverse gullies and ridges it seemed to us the best place on which to get lost. The excessive stoniness, and hence discomfort, of our present mountain tracks is the principal change in the fells from fifty years ago. Walking was so much more pleasant in earlier days. Of course, the modern rehabilitation of footpaths had not started fifty years ago and the paths were much the same as they had been before the war.

It should be remembered, too, that 1951 was four years before Alfred Wainwright wrote the first of his splendid illustrated *Pictorial Guide to the Lakeland Fells – The Eastern Fells* (published by my old friend, Harry Marshall, from his home, Low Bridge in Kentmere, which used to be the local pub before it was closed because of the bad behaviour of its customers, mostly navvies working on the Kentmere Reservoir dam). So the new flood of interest in our mountains, sparked off by Wainwright's tireless initiative, had not yet started and the tracks were not grossly over-used, as they are today. Indeed, there were no walking guides to the Lake District in those days, other than the outdated and old-fashioned Baddeley and Ward Locke guides. Nowadays, the district is saturated with guides to every corner, all going over much the same ground as their predecessors. As a result, the Lake District must nowadays be the least 'wild' or 'secret' holiday area in Britain.

Fifty years ago, Dore Head screes provided a fast, safe exhilarating descent into Mosedale after the round of the

Horseshoe or a day on Pillar Rock, and was certainly the finest scree-run in the Lake District. How different from the ugly grossly eroded descent today. Wasdale Head had no huge car park, as it does today, and you would rarely see more than two or three cars parked in the hamlet. There was no public telephone in Wasdale and electricity had not yet reached many of the dales, including Wasdale and even Borrowdale, while very few farms had the facility. Farmers were still using horses for the ploughing; the tractor age had not yet started.

There was not much interest in winter mountaineering in the fells fifty years ago and a handful of us seemed to have the snows and the ice-filled gullies almost to ourselves. Skiing had started in the fells but numbers were small. At the end of 1951 I wrote that the year had been one of rainfall records, long dry periods, snow on the tops until early summer and a sad Easter with blizzards and many tragedies in the mountains. At least five people lost their lives on the Lakeland fells during this holiday period, two young girls being missing for weeks before their bodies were found. Despite smaller numbers going into the mountains in those days, there seemed to be a long succession of tragedies over the years.

But, in a sense, the Lake District went to sleep during the winter months – after the agricultural shows and the sports meetings had finished. Nowadays, the 'season' can last all year, with weekend traffic queues hardly lessening during the shorter days. There were perhaps half the present number of hotels in the Lake District fifty years ago, and maybe about a third of the cafes and restaurants of today. Eating out was not then the fashion it has become today, and the public houses and inns would have to wait for many years before bars became eating places. In those days you went to the pub for a drink.

Fifty years ago saw another series of attempts by young Donald Campbell to travel faster on water than any other man in the world. As usual, he met disappointment after disappointment and, a few moments after eventually topping Stanley Sayer's record speed, after a miraculous escape, saw his boat sink almost out of sight, with a great hole in her hull.

At one time, in the early 1950s, Campbell had Bluebird converted into a two-seater, with his chief mechanic, Leo Villa, seated in the right-hand cockpit, primarily to watch the instruments. Later, they were anxious about the planing of the boat and the bow-wave which Leo wanted to study from the shore, so I volunteered – or was dared, I can't now remember – to go in the boat with Donald for a couple of runs. It was a very exciting experience – just like sliding on ice, when the boat hit perfectly calm water. We did something like 125 miles an hour, when the American held world record was only a little over 140mph, and Donald told me I had become the ninth fastest man in the world on water, since only eight people had driven faster. Of course, I wasn't driving the boat but merely trying to read the instruments and not look too scared.

Then, on 4 January 1967, came the sad end when I saw my old friend somersault to his death on Coniston Water. I had watched every one of his record attempts in this country and had come to know Donald very well. A very brave man, indeed.

In many ways I regret the passing of the Lake District of fifty years ago – the quieter, less crowded days when everybody seemed to have more time than we do today. I don't like crowds and queues and noise and I'm grateful I was able to enjoy the fells in the days when you knew almost everybody you met on the crags and you could often have the mountains to yourself. After all, peace and quietude are what is needed in a mountain national park – not crowds, bustle and noise. But, even in modern Lakeland, I can always find unspoiled, quiet places – even on public holidays.

The other day, convalescing after an illness, I drove

around the 'back' of my house through the familiar lanes of Underbarrow, Crosthwaite and Winster and thought what a delightful, unspoiled area, free from traffic and no sign of the evils of mass tourism, with the hedges newly burgeoning into colour and, everywhere, the spring flowers peeping out. And, for much of the continued peace and quietude of places like this we have to be grateful to the Lake District Planning Authority for its vigilance in controlling unseemly development. Its first fifty years have been, on the whole – with a few mistakes – a triumph of patience, wisdom and tenacity.

And, for reflecting so much of the beauty and diversity of the area in words and pictures we should also be grateful to *Cumbria* magazine and wish it well for the future.

PART THREE

Fell and Rock Climbing Club – *Journal* articles

INSIDE INFORMATION
1953

Every morning when I peep outside to see if it has stopped raining I look northwest across my lawn and the busy main road and admire for a moment – except when the mists are down – the shapely profile of Ill Bell and, just beyond, the great broad shoulder of High Street. They are there now, boldly framed in my window, as I write, and I have only to glance up from my typewriter to see, just over a clump of larches, the top part of Rainsborrow Crag, beloved of foxes but a hopeless place for climbing. This afternoon, I notice, there are still two tiny patches of snow hanging below the High Street plateau.

Tomorrow we will be going climbing as usual. From my house we can be on the climbs in White Ghyll in less than an hour and I have been on Buckbarrow in lonely Longsleddale in just over half an hour. Even the Wasdale hills are only two hours away.

And sometimes the fells seem nearer still. There was one afternoon less than a month ago when I dropped my skis over the back garden wall and trudged easily on skins all the way to the top of the fell. Ten minutes later as I topped the last rise there was the sudden glorious view of the whole of Alpine Lakeland – the Scafells, the Coniston fells, the Langdale Pikes, the Kentmere tops and many more – sparkling in the afternoon sunshine. There was not a soul about, not a mark on the snow except my own, and it was very still and very, very lovely. Then a train whistled on its way to Windermere and, turning around and looking down, I could see the smoke rising straight up from the chimneys and, underneath the old castle on the hill, the Town Hall clock. Half an hour after stealing out I was back – after the usual falls – at my garden wall, having seen the snows on Scafell Pike and the dark towers above Langdale.

All these joys, and many more, are possible because I

have the great good fortune to live on the edge of the Lake District. When you come to think about it our Club can be said to consist of two different types of member – those who live in the district or are so near that they can see the hills every day if they chose, and those to whom the Lake Country can never be more than a place of happy holidays, even although these holidays may occur every weekend. According to the latest list of members only about 135 of us are fortunate enough to be in the first category – something like one-seventh of the total membership – so that to the vast majority of members the Lake District must appear as a happy hunting ground, far enough away to be a complete change from their normal environment, a place of wonderful memories to which they return as often as they can.

But what does the Lake District mean to a member who lives either in its midst or on its borders? Can it possibly mean the same to him as it does to the man who has planned his weekend in the hills for perhaps months in advance, who leans out of his carriage window somewhere north of Carnforth hoping to catch his first glimpse of the fells? I can remember, during a long exile from the district, looking out for the first limestone outcrops which told me that industrial Lancashire was behind, and when I reached Levens Bridge I used to feel I was home again. Then, further on, there were the first views of Windermere, the glimpse, from near the Low Wood Hotel of the Langdale Pikes, looking surprisingly jagged, the sight of old, lichen covered, drystone walls, perhaps a few Herdwicks browsing among the boulders, and, when one stopped to fill up with petrol or tobacco, the old familiar dialect.

I can remember how I used to count the days before the chosen weekend, listen anxiously to weather forecasts, check up my equipment over and over again, and read up the climbs we had planned to do until I knew the descriptions by heart. Life was a series of exciting weekends strung together with long days of almost unbearable boredom in between.

For fourteen years the Lake District was a dream country anything from 70 to a few thousand miles away. Sometimes I could go back there for a quick weekend, but always there was the sad drive southwards in the evenings with a last glance back from the top of Bannerigg at the purpling hills backed by the setting sun.

When I came back again a few years ago – for good I hope – I wondered whether the old, nostalgic love would fade, and for a little time I felt almost shy of taking up the old familiar threads again, lest they should wither and snap in my hands.

Naturally, much of the old excitement has gone, but something else has taken its place. I no longer count the days to the weekend nor memorise the descriptions of climbs, but it is quite remarkable how the well known scenes still retain their charm. I suppose I travel beside the waters of Windermere at least four or five times every week – sometimes a dozen times – yet the other morning the almost hackneyed view across the lake was so breathtaking I had to stop and feast my eyes upon it for five minutes. It was early morning, and the water so calm that a bird alighting on the surface would have ruined the effect. A shadowy mist was hanging over the mere and through a gap in the slowly drifting curtain you could see the sun glinting on the distant rock turrets above Langdale.

Yes, the Lake Country is just as lovely even if seen every day, and there are so many sensations, experiences and sights to be enjoyed, so much knowledge to be won and discoveries to be made, besides the basic pleasures of climbing and fell walking. When I was an exile from my native Furness Fells the mountains meant everything, but nowadays, although rock climbing is just as attractive, there is so much else to enjoy – foxhunting on a crisp winter's morning, a green sports field in a hollow of the fells, the wrestling, the hound trails, the fell racing, the old Grasmere dialect plays (now, alas, only a memory), the sheepdog trials, the country dancing on a sunlit lawn of a summer's evening, the happy, colourful rushbearing festivals, the village choirs, sailing a dinghy on Windermere, skiing on Harter Fell, skating on a moonlit Tarn Hows, joining in the choruses at the Troutbeck shepherds' meet – oh, and a hundred-and-one other things.

Always there is something new to learn – the ways of the raven, the peregrine and the kestrel, the life of the mountain plants and the glory of the changing colours of the trees around the old quarry, the many differences between the Herdwick, the Swaledale and the Rough Fell, the problem of the bracken marching up the fellsides and the struggles and joys in a farmer's year, the old mines long since derelict, and the miners of centuries ago, the forgotten bloomeries on the lake shore, the holes where Lanty Slee made his whisky and the old paths that Moses Rigg knew so well, the story of the rocks and the meaning of the clouds, the red deer and the fell ponies, the Stone Age axes and the old stone walls winding over the fells, the unwritten lore of a dozen ancient crafts, the old local words and their meanings, the contribution the Norsemen made – the list is endless.

To a climber who lives near the fells there is the excitement and interest of finding new crags in remote, little visited dales – perhaps not major crags, but crags unscratched and too far away from the bars and the main roads to interest this strange new breed of mountaineers who are not interested in mountains. Without much difficulty I can think of half a dozen minor valleys in the Lake District, unmentioned in any climbing guide, where there is rock for climbing – perhaps not routes like those on the Pinnacle Face, but climbs worth doing all the same. There is one valley within a circle of 10 miles radius centred on the summit of Kirkstone Pass – I must not be more explicit for fear of giving the show away – where there is a magnificent, sensational traverse of 'very severe' standard embracing the entire width of an unexplored crag, which is quite unlike anything anywhere else in the district, and is waiting to be led. Two of us spent many Sundays at the place without success – my leader would have fared better with another second – but as far as I know nobody else has been there, before or since. And there are many other possibilities, even in the once very popular Coniston area. The lovely, unspoiled Deepdale where the buzzards soar was almost completely unknown to climbers until very recently, although one of the crags is only a few yards away from the walkers' route over Fairfield, and the perfect Vale of Newlands was surprisingly neglected until Eel Crags was opened up.

And then there are the characters of the district – the little old cobbler stolidly knocking nails into hikers' boots, who has climbed Liathach on a winter's day, seen three Brocken Spectres and knows the fells better than I know my back garden; the tough rock climber from one of the inner dales who knows and loves the birds, the flowers and the trees as well as the scholar knows his books; the lively old rascal still hunting at eighty, and the quaint little man in an old straw hat who has seen eighty Ambleside rushbearings; the very old gentleman with the silvery hair, the light steps and the courtly manners enjoying himself with the youngsters at the folk dancing; the famous general in charge of the turnstile; the foxhunter with more successes than John Peel; the expert on making shepherds' sticks and the man who makes violins; the dalesmen showing me where the fox cubs had danced and waiting with guns at the ready for the terriers to bolt the fox from the borran below Esk Buttress; the rough farmer's lad with the lovely, tenor voice at the shepherds' meet sing-song; the inborn artistry of the little lad of eight at the stone walling contest, and a hundred more.

There is so much to see in a Lakeland year when the fells are all around you – little things which may be missed when one is in the district for rock climbing alone. To say the fells look different every day is not an outworn platitude but a wonderful truth which the resident will notice if he has the eyes to see. And there is so much to learn – facts, background, history, weather and nature lore – that none of us will ever know the whole.

At random I dip into my notes of a Lakeland year seen from the inside, and the memories come quickly flooding back. There was the stolen hour of skiing on a January afternoon, with the sun sinking down towards the sea, the estuary dancing in the distant sunshine, and the old grey town smoking in the valley at our feet. Then, a day or two later, a chat with the old waller, kneeling in the snow to finish off his prize-winning section of wall at the local competition, and, on the last day of the month the sight for five long minutes of an arrogant fox, taking a leisurely stroll across his homeland fells, and, the same afternoon, the red deer climbing out of Riggindale on to High Street and the black-maned shaggy fell ponies quietly grazing just below the 2,500 feet contour line.

In February I remember the quarrymen opening up the old quarry among the larches and the silver birch which Lanty Slee knew so well and the shrill whirr of the diamond cutter as they rived the lovely sea green slate – the best, they say, in England. I remember the day when two of us found the site of the old smuggler's still deep down in the darkness, and the thrill when we discovered the ash from his fires, the bits of old barrel hoop, and even a piece of his clay pipe. The same month there were the merry sounds of the tree felling and hedge laying as well as the lorry drivers marooned in their cabs at night in the snows on Shap Fells. March brought the first lambs in the southern dales, the bird nesters secretly combing the crags for ravens' eggs, the practice hound trails on the lower fells, cheerful twelve year olds handling tractor ploughs at the local competitions, and a terrible battle between two game terriers and a most determined old badger. In April there was the glory of the damson blossom on a thousand trees in the Lyth Valley and, in May, the early morning fox hunts, fishing for char on Coniston Water and sailing a dinghy on Windermere with loose jib sheets and a limp racing flag on a calm evening perfect for everything except sailing.

Then June and the lazy, communal clipping with the country meals in the kitchen, and July with the folk dance festival, the sheepdog trials, a visit to the stone axe 'factory' and another to the radar station on the top of Great Dun Fell, and the joy of a bathe on the hottest day of the year in the deepest pool in Eskdale. And so the year goes on – August and the rushbearing with the television cameras and old Joe Grizedale in his fifty years old straw hat, Dog Day at Patterdale with the sheepdogs, the terriers and the trail hounds as well as the fancy shepherds' sticks. Grasmere, with the fell races, the brave music, the wrestling and a hundred familiar faces, and September with the sheep brought down for the dipping, and the huntsman out again in his bright red coat. October brings the colours, the bracken harvest, small boys already hauling bonfire material along the lane and perhaps an exploration of the old barites mine. In November we talk sheep at the shepherds' meet and sing '*The Mardale Hunt*' at the tattie-pot dinner, and as the year finishes, we may be skating around the frozen tarn which minutes earlier had borne the weight of a fleeing fox, and, nearer the edge, the scurrying of a frightened mountain mouse.

A thousand sights, adventures and discoveries in a single year – and a thousand more next year if we care to seek them out – with enough new beauty to last for a lifetime. The nearer one can live to the centre of Lake District life the more worthwhile the search for beauty; the nearer one is to the hills, the lovelier they appear. How fortunate those who live within the shadow of the fells. What a heritage to guard and to share.

INNOCENTS IN THE EAST
1955

The busy Kendal to Keswick artery through the Lake District and its continuation along the north shore of Bassenthwaite Lake towards Carlisle, cuts the National Park and its mountains into two approximately equal portions, and the layman might assume, if he was sufficiently interested, that it does much the same thing for the rock climbs of the district.

Climbers, however, know differently. West of the main road, with its double-decker buses, caravan sites and flourishing ice cream trade, there are listed, in half a dozen stout guidebooks, between 600 and 700 rock climbs, and many more routes still await official recognition. In the neglected eastern area, however – a reasonably hilly area which contains the Helvellyn range, Skiddaw, Blencathra, Fairfield, High Street and many more elevated sections of countryside – the climbs are easily contained in one modest section at the end of the old Dow Crag and Langdale guide, published in 1938. Even including obscure routes which have since proved unidentifiable the grand total is – or was – the miserable one of thirty-eight.

No doubt there are geological reasons why there should be more rock climbs west of Dunmail Raise than east of it but it seems strange that there should be as many as seventeen times more. You have only to examine the head of Deepdale or spend half an hour with your eyes open near the Thirlmere dam to realise that even these despised eastern fells can run to rock now and again. Moreover, many of the crags stand bare and bold on the fellside instead of lying hidden in the undergrowth or jungle like certain crags in a well-known western valley.

If you care to look for it there is, in fact, any amount of rock among the eastern fells, although some of these crags may only be reached by walking, which may not suit everyone. There are also several beautiful and, so far, almost deserted valleys, comparatively free of tracks, orange peel and litter. At the moment you can climb on these crags without the need for queuing, watch the buzzards soaring undisturbed or bathe in the pools without considering the proprieties – an idyllic state of affairs which doubtless will soon change when the new guide comes out. It will probably contain something like three times as many climbs as the old one – a modest increase occasioned, not by the authors, but by the commendable exploratory instincts of a small group of much tougher climbers.

The original authors of the 'Outlying Crags' section of the old guide were C. J. Astley Cooper and E. Wood-Johnson, but this was by no means their principal literary task at that time. The former had been rather more intimately involved with the Gable guide and the latter with the Borrowdale guide – in pre-Bentley Beetham days. Apparently, in the very beginning the word 'Borrowdale' was held to include 'all outlying climbs between Shap and the sea not provided for under the main crags'. Had Beetham been told this before embarking on his new Borrowdale guide there would now be climbs on John Bell's Banner and Wansfell Pike, great evidence of tree felling over most of Westmorland, and no need for this article.

Faced with the addition to their already considerable labours of completing the outlying crags section of the guide and trembling at the thought, as Astley Cooper put it in the 1933 *Journal*, that they might be saddled with researches into 'the basalt cliffs of Northumberland or the mouldering ironstone of the Cleveland hills' the early joint authors did not waste any time peering up untracked valleys for new climbs or signs of old ones but rushed into print as quickly as possible.

That was also the idea of G. B. Spenceley when he was detailed to investigate what another seventeen years had done to the outlying crags but he has been thwarted at every turn by people increasingly keen on scaling vertical or even overhanging rock. As I live in the district and have transport I was enrolled as assistant and at first we innocently thought the task might not be too formidable. We were aware that some climbers had discovered the existence of eastern Lakeland, but we took much comfort from the assurance of Astley Cooper that guidebook writers 'need not be brilliant exponents of the art of rock climbing, provided that they can call upon others to carry out the difficult routes.' We therefore cast about for people who could not only do 'very severes' but could also record what they had done in readable English.

Having thought of someone who might be able to drag us up some of the less overhanging things on the Castle Rock of Triermain and, having actually ascended Hangover on Dove Crag at the end of a very reliable nylon rope, we thought we might be able to press on with the 'difficults' with some confidence. But we were in for a rude shock.

One evening I happened to be tending my front lawn, which abuts on to the main road through the Lake District, and idly wondering whether we might be able to rise to a couple of 'very difficults' on Carrock Fell the following day when Donald Hopkin, laden with rope and travelling northwards, stopped his motorcycle at my gate. Glad of the excuse I abandoned my mower and we talked shop. He was on his way, he told me, to Raven Crag and, thinking he meant the Langdale one, I felt on familiar ground. Oh, yes, we'd cleaned up most of that, I boasted, but of course it was not an outlying crag. "It most certainly is," he countered, "I mean Raven Crag, Thirlmere. That's where the real climbers go now. There are nine V.S's there already."

This ruined our weekend. We had always known Raven Crag, Thirlmere, but had automatically written it off as much too steep for our attention. Now people had actually started climbing on the wretched thing and, although it lies a few hundred yards to the west of my quite arbitrary line of cleavage between western and eastern Lakeland, it was held to be an 'outlying crag.' "Marvellous routes, too," went on Hopkin, who I was beginning to like less every minute. "When we'd finished with Castle Rock we just moved across to the other side of the dam. Very convenient, really."

That sort of thing has been going on, I am sorry to say, ever since we started and my manager now authorises me to invite climbers who can do overhangs to come to our aid. We may even be able to get them a mention in the new guide.

To counter this distressing accent on verticality and to find something we could do, George and I once discovered a new crag, Eagle Crag in Grisedale, after watching a nimble sheep accomplishing the last few feet of what looked a pleasant climb. We thought that if a sheep could get up there must be holds on it and we might even be able to get up ourselves. The result was three quite nice, sunny routes, a couple of possible routes which better climbers might be able to polish off and a fearsome looking thing which Jim Birkett thought might go on a good day. Seeing that none of us could even get off the ground on this route we did not even bother to inspect the overhangs higher up on a rope.

Of course, our principal concern has been sorting out the older routes. The oldest of them – apart from Iron Crag Gully in Shoulthwaite, which dates back to the heroic era and should be written off – is Dollywaggon Gully, climbed by Col. Westmorland when he was a little lad and probably never repeated until our ascent generations later. That was our impression at the time, anyway. This gully is now rather safer than before, large portions of its retaining walls having peeled off during our ascent. This was a climb which we felt might be within our powers – it was classified 'moderately difficult' – but as it was rather a wet day we employed Jack Carswell to lead the enterprise. At one point, I discovered that the wall against which I was negligently leaning was about to collapse. George, who was below me, had to do some urgent scampering before I could step to one side and allow the force of gravity to replenish the screes below.

For some reason, I seem to have been considerably involved with loose rock in recent years. One occasion, not concerned with this guide, was when Eric Arnison inconsiderately dropped a large rock on me in Newlands Gully on Miners' Crag. I did not see the thing coming down but it felt exactly like being crushed by a heavy sideboard. Eric shouted down, "Tie yourself on in case you faint, and sit down for a bit." I was trying to comply with the instructions when he dropped another one on me. I saw this one coming, but being a sitting bird there was not much I could do about it, and he winged me on the arm.

Oddly enough Eric was also involved in some rock juggling on Migraine on Hutable Crag in Deepdale. It was my turn to lead and I was pedalling about in a little crack quite a way above the screes without making much progress. Eric was 20 feet below me, and as I was making heavy weather of it he kindly came up and took a fragmentary belay just below me. I then made my effort, reached up for the top of a jammed flake – and the whole mass lurched outwards.

Several things then happened very quickly. Eric reached up and pressed me onto the rock, just holding me in balance, I managed to hold the flake in place for a second or two with my knee and George, who was supervising from the screes, was told to get himself and Eric's dog out of it as quickly as possible. This took about three seconds but it seemed like three hours. At the end of it a few tons of flake hurtled to the screes. We all had another look at the crack, both from below and from above, and decided – greatly to my relief – that I had so wrecked the pitch that it was now quite impossible. The route now goes to the left.

One of the disadvantages of being assistant to a guide writer is that on unsavoury routes you have to do all the dirty work, leaving him to his writing in the comparatively comfortable position of second man. This mostly happens in dirty gullies and the literary work is carried out on miserable bits of notepaper which are completely bedraggled and unreadable at the end of the day. This casual approach to creative work is to be deplored. I once received, through the post, a missive from Spenceley and Tom Price, then holidaying in Skye, which consisted of the sodden side of a Quaker Oats packet, date-lined 'The Howff, Coruisk, Monday', with the message more or less obliterated either by spray, paraffin or both. On the pleasanter routes the manager probably insists on leading as many of the best pitches as you will allow, and the assistant's job then becomes largely a question of trying to remember how many pieces of white tape – tied on the rope at 5 feet intervals – have passed him by.

Now and again a conscientious guidebook writer feels himself compelled to investigate one of the harder routes – even if he has to be dragged up by a minion – but an assistant can plead loss of form or indifferent footgear and wriggle out of the duty. George felt himself impelled for some extraordinary reason to check the already excellent description of Hangover on Dove Crag and secured a young 'tiger' to do the hard work. I felt no urge whatever to attempt this overhanging cliff but I promised to walk up the screes and shout directions. Having thus washed my hands of the whole affair I spent the day before the attempt in motoring some very active young men about the Lake District. They were pacing an even more active and younger man on an attempt to break Bob Graham's fell running record. As two of the pacers had to cover between them nearly all the Lake District mountains this meant quite a day, even for the motorist. Weather interfered with the attempt but that was no reason for cancelling the celebration which followed, and the party finished in the early morning hours.

The screes below Dove Crag are steep, but the next morning they were nearly vertical and I was very relieved to reach the foot of the crag where I hoped to sit and gloat. Most unfortunately, however, this was not to be. Despite the promises that had been made, supported by every excuse I could manufacture, I was eventually bullied into tying on. The thing which really clinched the matter was that the young man who had run up and down about twenty mountains the previous day was also to be taken up the climb by one of his pacers. After that, it was useless saying anything.

All I can say about the climb is that the crux seemed to be both strenuous and delicate at one and the same moment, and that nylon rope is extremely reliable. I would have thought that the leader would have been demoralised by the discovery of the piton lying at the foot of the climb – the longest and rustiest one we had ever seen, something like a large piece of railing. However, he had more of his own and, later on, hanging from one of his pieces of ironmongery at the friction stance, I marvelled at the wonders of engineering and thought longingly of the comfortable grass ledge below me on the screes where I had planned to sleep and smoke. Afterwards we all agreed it was a magnificent climb – it was certainly a very fine lead.

There is much more to be done among the eastern fells – maybe not climbs like Hangover, but probably pleasant routes for the average climber in rather different country. These new routes need not include the '30 foot moderates' which Astley Cooper so despised twenty-two years ago, but there may be several 150 feet 'very difficults' for the picking. Such routes are not to be discounted – as one grows older they become more and more attractive – and they would be even better if twice as long. Certainly something has been done on a smallish scale to offset the weekend congestion in Langdale and Borrowdale and no doubt the work will continue. Perhaps this is a selfish thought, but I only hope the eastern fells will not become *too* crowded.

NOSTALGIA FOR NAILS
1981

There are probably one or two remarkable members of the Club who have some recollection, if only slight, of climbing in the Lake District in those peaceful, happy days seventy-five years ago when the Fell and Rock was formed, and no doubt a few whose memories go back for seventy years. Many members, of course, can clearly recall climbing sixty or more years ago so that these scattered reminiscences, by an undistinguished mountaineer, of Lakeland climbing a mere half-century or so ago must be regarded as commonplace, if not almost impertinent. Indeed, my only qualifications as a climbing historian are that my memory of early days is often clearer than that of much more recent events, that I started rock climbing fifty-three years ago – although my Club membership only extends to a mere forty-eight years – and that, living in the district, I am fortunately still able to potter about fairly regularly in my own fashion.

What wonderful spacious days they were in the late 1920s and early 1930s – carefree, youthful days on uncrowded crags, so long before even the threat of war. Outside holiday times the Lake District, in those uncomplicated days, could still be regarded as a quiet, fairly secluded paradise with few motor cars, no caravan sites or litter baskets, uneroded tracks and the four-in-hands going over the passes. You could sit on top of Pillar Rock and look down the long length of Ennerdale without seeing a tree, Mardale Green was still a peaceful, old-world oasis among the fells, and Millican Dalton, Professor of Adventure, was living in his cave on Borrowdale's Castle Crag. When I first took to the rocks there were no climbing huts or youth hostels in Lakeland – the Robertson Lamb Hut in Langdale was opened by the Wayfarers Club in 1930 – no telephone at Wasdale Head, and no cars on the roadside below Shepherd's Crag. Indeed, apart from an early ascent of Brown Slabs Arête by

Bentley Beetham and Claude Frankland this crag, and many more of our modern crags, had not even been 'discovered'. There were fewer than 300 classified rock climbs in the Lake District; today there are at least 3,000. And few people in England had even heard of Adolf Hitler.

Several of the original pioneers, the men who had practically invented the sport of rock climbing in Lakeland, were still fairly active. Cecil Slingsby, father of our beloved Eleanor Winthrop Young, died in 1929 but names like those of Collie, Bruce and Geoffrey Hastings were still among our honorary members and, on occasions, I was privileged to encounter the 'Father of British Climbing', Haskett-Smith, with his curious, long coat, fierce moustache and gift of ready repartee. Godfrey Solly, with his great white beard, the man who first led Eagle's Nest Direct in 1892, was sometimes to be seen at Club meets and George Abraham, still erect and slim, I came to know him quite well. And I remember too, long before the war watching Geoffrey Winthrop Young climbing one of the Dow Crag buttresses, led, I think, by George Bower, with a third man helping the distinguished second to raise his metal leg onto the holds.

Climbing standards had clearly risen by the late 1920s, since the early assaults on the gullies and chimneys, but clothes, equipment and techniques had not vastly changed from those that had been in use in the pioneering days, while the number of climbers and clubs can hardly have been one-tenth of today's total, and perhaps much less than this. Climbers were still regarded as unusual if not slightly eccentric people, and ropes – almost the only badge of the sport at that time – had often to be explained away or hidden in the rucksack. One quite common misconception among the general public was that you swarmed up the rope – perhaps after hurling it up to loop over a spike. The media – fortunately, perhaps – had not discovered climbing. Perhaps hang-gliders have similar difficulties today in their public relations. The hardest climb, by far, in Lakeland in the 1920s was Central Buttress; and since its first ascent in 1914 it had only been twice repeated. 'Very severes' were, of course, the ultimate achievement – one trained for them on boulders – and we accorded them a proper respect, only tackling them when we felt on top form and, even then, being prepared to retreat if they proved too hard. After all, you couldn't put in a nut for security, or to rest, in those days.

Strangely, one of the hardest climbs in Langdale at that time was E Route on Gimmer – years later, so quickly had standards risen, we were to use it occasionally as a convenient descent route – although I well remember the considerable breakthrough made by Hargreaves and Macphee's ascent of Deer Bield Crack in 1930, first described by them as merely severe. Only fifteen climbs were listed in the Borrowdale area fifty years ago – a section originally tacked on to the end of the first Great Gable guide. 'The climbs in Borrowdale', stated the introduction to this guide, 'are few and far between'. Today, there are at least 400 of them.

When I began climbing in the late 1920s there were a few family bases or weekend cottages scattered throughout the district but, with no climbing huts available, climbers mostly stayed in hotels or farmhouses for camping was not so nearly as popular as it is today. The Wastwater Hotel, under John and Sally Whiting, was the centre of Lake District climbing, while the Edmondson sisters in Buttermere and the Jopsons at Thornythwaite in Borrowdale provided comfortable, homely accommodation, as did many farmhouses. At Coniston the Sun Hotel was the main centre before Mrs Bryan and Miss Pirie opened their accommodation for climbers at Parkgate, while Mrs Harris's cottage was always a home from home. In Langdale, John Dawson was at the Old Dungeon Ghyll Hotel, the Forthergills at the New and the Grisedales at Middlefell Farm.

Each summer, in my early years I was fortunate enough to spend my holidays at the Wastwater Hotel with George Basterfield (President 1929-31) and, being in such distinguished company, was warmly received by the Whitings. They, with Edie Long, were always extremely kind to me, mending my socks and trousers and once, I remember, when badly sunburned, treating my back with calamine lotion. Lake District hotel prices in those days were usually about ten shillings for dinner, bed and breakfast or a guinea for the weekend from Saturday evening dinner to Monday morning breakfast. But I think the Whitings put me on a special cheap rate for my holidays, since I was a protégé of George, and even accorded me the rare distinction, reserved for really important guests, of evening coffee in the 'office'. The Whitings, however, could be difficult with some people – often for unaccountable reasons. I remember once being approached by H. G. Knight, Kelly's companion on Grooved Wall, Pillar and several routes on Great Gable, who explained he was camping near Ritson Force, would like to look at some Club *Journals* in his tent, but he had been denied access by the Whitings to the Club bookcase in the hotel. Could I please smuggle something out for him? This was done although I was fearful of Sally Whiting's wrath if the subterfuge was detected.

Portraits of Will Ritson and Owen Glynne Jones, with dozens of other pictures of climbs and climbers, adorned the dining room walls, the hall was full of boots, ropes and ice axes, and a chest on the stairs could always provide you with spare socks, shirt or trousers in an emergency. I remember the conversion of the famous billiards room into a modern lounge and listening to George Basterfield picking out the melodies on the piano, with two fingers, for his *Songs of a Cragsman*. In the evenings I used to sit, a raw youngster, at the feet of the great men in the tiny smoking room, listening to their tales and sometimes joining in the songs.

One of the regulars at the hotel at that time was A. E. Field, a quiet, scholarly figure, the companion of Jones and George Abraham on the epic first ascent of Walker's Gully in 1899. He was pictured on the dining room wall, wearing old-fashioned tweeds and nailed boots, on the slightly sloping holds of Eagle's Nest Direct – an Abraham picture that had always fascinated and slightly terrified me – and it was a delight to meet the man himself. Sometime later I was encouraged to lead the climb by Basterfield, who, as my second, made it all seem much easier than the photograph. One year I was fortunate enough to have a week's climbing from Wasdale with George Sansom, Herford's companion on the first ascent of Central Buttress, who took me up, among many other climbs, my first 'very severe', North West on Pillar.

Another of the Wasdale company in those days was C. F. Holland, author of the first Scafell guide and climbing companion of both Herford and Kelly. Holland was deeply affected by the death of Herford during the First World War and believed that sometimes he met his spirit in the fells – on one occasion, an almost personal encounter. One very wet and cloudy day Holland, Basterfield and I, on our way to climb on Pillar Rock, were sheltering on Black Sail Pass when a man with a bicycle on his back suddenly loomed out of the mist and asked us if he was "on the right road to Whitehaven?", Holland enjoyed that. The Wastwater Hotel always seemed to be full of professors and other learned men in those days. One of them was said to complete the difficult 'Torquemada' crossword puzzle in *The Observer*, without reference books, on each visit.

My introduction to 'proper' climbing had been provided by George Basterfield, that kindliest of men who must have started off scores of novices. Before he took me in hand I had been exploring a small ironstone crag on The Hoad at Ulverston . It seemed important to get my cheap ex-army boots nailed but I had no idea how to go about it. The only local climber of whom I was aware – by name and reputation only – was George Basterfield who happened to be the Mayor of Barrow at the time. So, plucking up my courage, I went to see the great man in the Mayor's

Parlour to ask his advice and George not only told me how to get my boots nailed – by George Stephens at Coniston – but actually offered to take me climbing on Dow Crag the following Sunday. Today, fifty-three years later, I can clearly remember every incident of that first day. On the way up to the Crag from the old quarries at Tranearth above Torver, George pointed out many of the routes on the cliff and, somewhere near the quartz chain, stopped, looked at the ground and told me, with confidence, who would be climbing that day. In those days climbers used distinctive types of nailing – sometimes with nails of their own manufacture – and George, studying the imprints of the nails on the track, knew exactly who we would meet on the crag. To a youngster, this smacked of magic.

He took me up Woodhouse's – getting me to lead the awkward top pitch on my very first climb – down Easter Gully, up Arête, Chimney and Crack and down Great Gully. On our way down Great Gully we joined up with A. T. Hargreaves and Bill Clegg – I think they'd been 'looking at' Eliminate A – and, after introductions, George quietly confided to me that these two were up-and-coming 'tigers' – the first time I had encountered this use of the word. Later I came to know both these fine climbers very well. The day proved even more rewarding and exciting than I anticipated. I can clearly remember, for instance, looking down between my legs at the screes while climbing the final crack on A Buttress and thinking that this was the most wonderful experience of my young life. All at once, climbing seemed the only thing that mattered. Thereafter, I was on Dow Crag almost every weekend, sometimes with George but more often alone – hanging about at the foot of the cliff, with the cheek and confidence of youth, waiting for somebody to take me up a climb. No doubt I was a nuisance but several kind people took pity on me. I particularly remember the kindness of Mrs B. Eden-Smith, Kelly's partner on Moss Ghyll Grooves and other climbs, who took me up several routes. In those earliest days I had no rope, although very soon I was given a 50 foot length – severed, by a falling stone, from a longer length and handed over to me by an unknown climber who had no further use for it. I still have my tattered copy of Bower's red 'Doe Crag' guide with my list, written in ink on the last page – 'climbs possible with 50 foot rope'.

Gradually, climbing friends were made and nine of us from the Barrow and Ulverston area formed a club, which we eventually named, most inaccurately, the Coniston Tigers. Only one of us could have been called a tiger – Jim Porter, who once christened a new rope by trailing it after him in an evening solo ascent of Botterills'Slab, and who was the only one of us to lead Black Wall on Dow Crag. We had our own wooden hut, heated with a combustion stove, at Coniston Old Hall, near the lake shore, sleeping on rough camp beds we had made ourselves and having a weekend ritual of a dip in Coniston Water or Goat's Water, no matter what the weather. From this base we worked through the 'Doe Crag' guide and also did most of the Langdale climbs. The Napes, Scafell and Pillar were mostly reserved for summer holidays. This climbing hut of ours was almost the first in the Lake District. The Robertson Lamb might have opened about the same time, and Bill Clegg and Geoff Barker had a private hut somewhere on Wetherlam quite a long time before we opened ours. For most of us these days, long before the war, made up the happiest of our lives.

There must have been fewer than 100 people regularly climbing the Lake District crags fifty years ago – every weekend, I mean, not just in holidays – and we knew nearly all of them. Little groups of climbers from the Kendal, Keswick, Penrith, Barrow and Ulverston areas met frequently on the crags, and at holiday times there was an influx from the universities and elsewhere. Sid Cross was one of the regulars in the Kendal group and I remember first meeting our distinguished past president – a wild lad in those days – on Dow Crag at least fifty years ago. There was some friendly rivalry between these groups, each regarding their favourite crag as their own preserve. We felt we were almost intruders on the Napes or Scafell but reckoned we practically 'owned' Dow Crag.

The only guidebooks in those days were the excellent, red-backed guides published by the Fell and Rock in which Dow was written 'Doe' and Scafell Crag , 'Scawfell'. In those days 'Carter's celebrated climbing boots' were advertised at £4.12s.6d., including nailing. We used ordinary army boots, nailed by George Stephens for a few shillings. Years later I bought my first pair of Lawrie's boots but had to go to Burnley to get measured for them. On the harder climbs we wore cheap plimsolls – worn a size too small for a tighter fit. The best were black, with very thin soles, costing one and sixpence. We used Beale's 'Alpine Club' manilla hemp rope, with its red strand down the centre, although this got rather heavy and almost unmanageable when wet. Sometimes, on climbs, with long run-outs or small belays, we used line – partly to avoid the pull of a heavier rope which we must have thought more important than the safety of thickness. We had no slings or karabiners, no pegs, nuts or bits of wire. If a pitch was 80 or 100 feet long you ran out a length of rope without protection. The shoulder belay was universal – The Tarbuck knot had not been invented – and abseiling, without a sling, could be rather painful. If there was an accident you dealt with it yourself as best you could, for there were no rescue teams in those days. Everybody just rallied round. Sometimes, after an accident on Dow Crag, Bill Fury, the Coniston fireman, would bring a horse and cart as far as the shoulder below Goat's Water to ease the carry down the fell.

Developments in climbing equipment seemed to come very slowly. There were a few experiments with nails – some, you screwed in – and the waisted clinker, reducing the effective width of the nail, was hailed as a great step forward.

Robert Lawrie was an early pioneer of boots for climbers but the flood of footwear from abroad did not come until after the war and vibrams had not been invented. I think we climbed more often on wet rock than climbers do today, nailed boots being more suitable for these conditions, and longish walks over the fells often followed our climbs. Dare I say it, climbers were perhaps more all-round mountaineers than some of the rock gymnasts are today, for few roadside crags had been developed. Anoraks and climbing jackets did not come into general use until after the war. Mostly we used old tweed jackets, corduroy breeches and balaclavas and just got wet through if it rained. Sometimes, if we were trying something really hard, we wore white polo-neck sweaters because these showed up well on photographs. Once, when climbing with Graham Macphee on Gable Crag long before the war he showed me, with some pride, an anorak he had made out of an old mackintosh, with cunningly contrived cords to adjust its length. This seemed to me a significant development.

The outstanding climbers in the Lake District fifty or more years ago were probably H. M. Kelly and G. S. Bower although, by that time, both were drawing towards the end of their greatest achievements. Kelly, a daring pioneer on Pillar, Scafell and Great Gable, had written the first Pillar Rock guide and Bower, especially active on Dow Crag and in Langdale, the first Dow ('Doe') Crag guide – the first of the Club's guides to be published. I did not meet Harry Kelly until after the war but knew George Bower, so quiet-spoken and modest, from my earlier days. It was Bower who suggested the name for an early first ascent in which I took part just fifty years ago – Tiger Traverse on Dow Crag, led by Dick Mackereth of Ulverston with Bryan Tyson of Hawkshead as second – and, another first ascent the following weekend – Blasphemy Crack on Dow Crag – but, forced to change into nails because of heavy rain after the first two had gone up in rubbers, distinguished myself by falling off halfway up and finally abandoning the climb.

Other prominent pioneers at that time were H. S. Gross who wrote the first Great Gable guide – a serious gliding accident put an end to his climbing – G. Basterfield, G. G. Macphee, H. G. Knight, A. B. Reynolds (who often climbed in bare feet), Fergus Graham and the Wood-Johnson brothers. Just emerging as outstanding leaders were A. T. Hargreaves and Maurice Linnell who together opened up the possibilities of Scafell's East Buttress; J. A. Musgrave, who made a point of leading all the new hard climbs in nails; and F.G Balcombe whose routes included the splendid Engineer's Slabs on Gable Crag. It was to be another ten years before R. J. Birkett began to come into his own as the outstanding leader in the district. A. B. Hargreaves, more active in North Wales at this time, was, however, with Linnell on the girdle traverse of Pillar Rock and also on Esk Buttress, while Colin Kirkus, on a rare visit from his beloved Wales, put up the bold lead of Mickledore Grooves in 1931.

Other climbers remembered from my early days were A. R. Thomson, who wrote the first Borrowdale guide and had effected the remarkable rescue of Mr T. C. Crump from Piers Gill in 1921 after his eighteen days' ordeal, C. D. Yeomans, C. J. Astley-Cooper, A. W. Wakefield, Stanley Watson and Geoffrey Barker. Arthur Thomson, who used to bring over an Austrian guide as climbing companion, was one of the characters of the district. I once met him riding his bicycle up Dunmail Raise in great distress, standing on the pedals but refusing to dismount. Douglas Yeoman, who became an honorary member of the Club, often used to appear on Dow Crag where he would boast, jokingly, that he was "the oldest man leading severes". Astley-Cooper another kindly soul, once came to my aid when I had stupidly managed to get off route during an early lead of Abbey Buttress. Stan Watson was one of the early guides and Geoff Barker, an old friend from early Barrow days.

Winter climbing fifty years ago had not made any marked development since the early days. The Great End gullies were popular – in nailed boots, for crampons were rarely used – and sometimes we tried some of the easier Dow Crag routes in winter, including Woodhouse's which I suppose I must have climbed more often than any other route, in all conditions. It is a source of some satisfaction to old-timers like myself that dear old Woodhouse's has been upgraded since we first knew it – 'hard very difficult' now compared with merely 'difficult' in the clinker and manilla days. Other routes now graded as harder than when we did them in the late 1920s and early 1930s include Eagle's Nest Direct, Kern Knotts Crack and Smuggler's Chimney – all translated from 'severe' to 'very severe'. Napes Needle too has gone from 'difficult' to 'hard very difficult'.

There were no professional guides in the Lake District when I started climbing apart from friendly old Millican Dalton, the Borrowdale hermit, whom I often met wheeling his shopping on a lady's bicycle in Rosthwaite. For a small consideration he would take novices up the Needle, make you a tent or a rucksack or cook you a meal – for free – in his cave. J. E. B. Wright began his guiding, amid some opposition, in 1930 and Jim Cameron started in 1937. There were no outdoor pursuits centres, either, in those days; you just worked your way through the lists with a companion, learning the hard way.

Looking back on it all one feels immense gratitude for a lifetime of mountaineering – the physical, mental and even spiritual exhilaration, the excitements and splendours of the changing seasons and lasting friendships. I count myself extremely fortunate to have spent most of my life in my beloved Lakeland, to have climbed in quieter, less crowded days, to have met so many of the great men in our sport, and to be still able to enjoy the fells and the rocks in a modest fashion. Of course, confined nowadays to easy routes and rather bewildered by rapidly changing developments, the holds seem to have shrunk and moved farther apart, although just to scramble about on uncomplicated rock brings its rewards. But the climbing scene today, with 'very severes' the norm and 'extremes' beyond belief, is a world removed from our carefree adventuring of more than fifty years ago.

A SKI MOUNTAINEERING JUBILEE
1986

While we are celebrating a century of rock climbing in the Lakes it may be appropriate to notice the golden jubilee of skiing in the area. In January 1986 the Lake District Ski Club modestly celebrated, with a dinner and a club journal – only the second in its history – its fifty years' existence. The inaugural meeting of the club, shortly after New Year's Day,1936, was really the bringing together of a few small groups of Lake District ski mountaineers to share information about snow conditions and the best areas for the winter exploration of the fells. The occasional skier was seen on the fells in the early 1900s, and early last century the Glenridding miners are said to have descended from their mountain huts in wintertime on 'barrel staves'. Presumably, though, this desperate sounding expedient – did they have closing hours in those days? – was for convenience rather than sport.

As far as I am aware our Club played no official part in the formation of the Lake District Ski Club; 'our healthy relative' as one of our *Journals* put it. The early officers were largely Fell and Rock members; the formation and activities of the new club, especially in ski mountaineering, were reported upon at some length in several of our *Journals,* notably by Edmund Hodge; and our club was favourably disposed towards the upstart. Some climbers might look down their noses at skiers but not – at least at that time – the Fell and Rock. Perhaps this was partly because our esteemed

Leslie Somervell was the first president of the Lake District Ski Club, holding down the job for ten years, while Bentley Beetham, the first vice president, held unbroken office in that rank for twelve years. Rusty Westmorland succeeded Leslie Somervell as president of the ski club and other Fell and Rock members who served as president of the LDSC are Dick Cook, Eric Arnison, Bill Kendrick and the writer. Another Fell and Rock member, Jim Bannister, is the present vice president. John Appleyard was an early vice president, Edmund Hodge an early treasurer and would-be ski guide writer, and Phyllis Wormell secretary for some years. Molly Fitzgibbon served in several offices, almost continuously, for nearly thirty years.

The mountaineering flavour these names give to the ski club – and other Fell and Rock members have also been active in the LDSC – is perfectly understandable since, in the early days, piste skiing had not reached Britain, let alone the Lakes, and skiing was largely ski mountaineering; going up and down mountains on skis. To most of the early members of the new club skiing was an enjoyable alternative to ice axe work in the gullies and skis useful pieces of equipment for exploring the hills in winter. They fitted skis to their nailed boots, wore their ordinary mountain clothes, often carried axes for the steep, icy places and fastened on their skins – originally, sealskins – as soon as they reached the first snow. Even my own first skiing, about forty years ago, was in the same mould – primitive skis without steel edges fastened on to nailed climbing boots, after first gouging out grooves in the heels to take the elementary bindings, for an ascent and descent of Harter Fell from Longsleddale. The ascent, using skins – naturally, in those days, acquired at the same time as the skis – was straightforward enough but the descent, since I had no idea how to turn, quite disastrous – a succession of falls, all the way down. In retrospect, though, there had at least been the delightful sliding along the easy bit at the top and the dramatic views across winter Lakeland.

No doubt, on that distant day in the 1940s, a would-be ski mountaineer, with a very great deal to learn, emerged.

It used to be called ski touring in the early days and a few of us old stagers, more interested in mountains than in careering down the same bit of fellside, time after time – and, also, let it be admitted, no longer athletic enough for icy moguls – still prefer this sort of skiing and seek it out whenever there is general snow cover and we can summon up the necessary energy. For ski mountaineering certainly needs more continuous effort than ordinary piste skiing where as much time, or more, is spent in being whisked effortlessly up the slopes, not counting the time standing in the lift queues. Piste skiing is, or should be, neat and elegant and, in its higher flights demands considerable technical skill, but these skiers don't need to know anything about mountains or even about the vastly varied types of snow as the ski mountaineer does. To ski, away from the piste, the Lakeland fells, the Scottish hills, the Alps or any other mountains, completely and with enjoyment, it certainly helps considerably if you are a skilled technical skier, but an average skier with winter mountaineering experience will probably cope just as well. It is far more important, in the mountains, to be able to ski slowly, under complete control, while assessing the changing quality and suitability of the snow, as well as of the weather, than to be capable of fast, elegant descents. Many a mountaineer whose parallels or short swings leave much to be desired has skied the Haute Route.

Living within the Lake District National Park and retired now, for more than ten years, it is comparatively easy for me to seize ski mountaineering possibilities on the fells seen from my windows – or, more likely, others that might have better snow – whenever there is general snow cover or, at least, snow down to, say, 1,000 feet. The winter of 1984/1985 was one of the worst for skiing, any sort of skiing, in the Lake District for many years but at one time,

1. A. Harry Griffin, the young Coniston Tiger.

2. Courting in Lakeland, Harry and Mollie.

3. Coniston Tigers Hut (Harry, second from left).

4. Harry, the *Daily Mail* journalist.

5. Harry, army portrait.

6. Harry at Imphal during the Burma Campaign.

7.   Harry and brother Les. 1956.

8.   Harry at the Matterhorn.

9.   Arthur Griffin, Harry's father, on High Fell.

10. Harry climbing on Shepherds' Crag, Borrowdale.

11. A family picnic. Sandra, Mollie and Robin.

12. Harry skiing on Raise.

13. One of two RSPCA awards, presented in 1955 and 1957, for rescuing cragfast sheep.

14. Harry and Mollie, official opening of The Griffin Bar, Beech Hill Hotel, Windermere. 1969.

15. Sambo, Harry's companion on the Fells.

16. Sgurr Alasdair, Skye.

17. Harry, sailing off Vancouver, Canada. 1984.

19. Harry, 91 years of age. 2002.

18. Harry, wedding day to his second wife Violet. 1989.

June 11.

A.H.G. went To Wasdale for a week &, renewed acquaintance with many good friends, & made some new ones. Most of the Napes climbs & the Nose (North) & West Wall on Pillar were led & he was led up North. West by G.S. Sansom.

With LKG. an

20. Coniston Tigers Log Book detailing a trip to Wasdale.
Climbing with G.S. Sansom.

At the hut, everything was progressing on sound lines. Golf seemed to be the reigning passion, G.A and D.B proving sound exponents, while others, of the calibre of the scribe, merely lost the balls.

However, in one glorious swing, A.H.G., doubtless by a "fluke", managed to hole out in one at the third "hole", in a round with T.T.

21. Coniston Tigers Log Book. Notes on playing golf.

Aug 1st. Long Sleddale. Scrambling route to Kentmere Pike to the right of Goat Scar. Harter Fell & Adam Seat. (28)

Aug. 8 Up Short Stile on to Rampsgill, High Raise, Low Raise. (Found post.) (29) Very close

Aug. 15 (with Mollie & Stacey's) from Carrock Mine - Carrock fell, High Pike, Coomb Height. Good, easy day. (30)

Aug 22 (approx)

Langdale. Tarn Crag, Sretch Rake, Thunacar Knott, Pike O'Stickle, Gimmer (to meet climbers), Very hot. (31)

Aug 29 (approx)

Watson's Dod from Stanah. Great Dod. Down Stanah Gill (litter) Very hot. (31)

22. A page from Harry's walking diary. August 1981.

four months of weekend skiing – even if only shortish drifts high in the fells could be expected and the fells have been skied as early as November and as late as May – and, in 1979, in the middle of June, a few days before Midsummer's Day. But ski mountaineering, needing a fair blanket of snow on the fells, is not normally feasible for anything like as long as ordinary downhill skiing and the opportunities have to be quickly seized as they occur.

There are obvious places such as the round of the Dodds, the Helvellyn range, the Skiddaw- Blencathra area, the Fairfield Horseshoe, the High Street fells, the Howgill fells and so on but sometimes it has been rewarding to get on the skirts of Bowfell around The Band or on the Easedale edges or, better still and potentially best of all, on to Esk Hause and the Scafells. The traverse of the Coniston heights can be good and, occasionally, quite unlikely seeming places like Blea Rigg or Red Screes have proved enjoyable and even the steep slopes above Helvellyn's Red Tarn have been descended on skis. It was the unusual sight, at that time, of skiers descending from High Raise to Grasmere in long elegant turns that first inspired me to try the game but I soon found that the slow ascent of any steepish fellside, using skins, working out the best line through different or craggy terrain, can be, as in a fell walk or climb, just as important, and sometimes as interesting, as the descent. Even to climb Caudale Moor from Kirkstone Pass on skis, descending by a different route, is infinitely preferable to an afternoon cavorting down the slopes near the inn, in company with shrieking sledgers and maniacal cagoule glissaders. And a quiet traverse along the Helvellyn ridge, ticking off the tops, is usually more enjoyable than a dozen or so runs down Savage's Drift on Raise – with the help of the tow – in much the same grooves that people have been using for at least forty years now.

Skiing the tops one is usually either alone or with a chosen companion, seeking out the way in untracked snows;

on the piste, you are generally with dozens, even scores, of others, either queuing for the lift or tow or trying to get out of one another's way on the descent. On the tops one can enjoy one's thoughts, the scenery or the intricacies of the route in silence, with, perhaps, the occasional monosyllabic grunt; on the piste you sometimes might just as well be in a funfair.

I remember once skiing, with a friend, several of the Cairngorm 'four-thousanders' on the most perfect day for powder snow, weather and sunshine I can ever remember enjoying in Britain, seeing nobody else and finishing off with the swoop down the Lurcher's Gully and the traverse across the floor of the corries. As we reclined in the heather on the Fiacaill Ridge after our long round we looked down at the scurrying ants on the White Lady and in Coire Cas, listening to the distant rattle of machinery and the cries of colliding skiers. One of us asked; "What about a couple of quick runs?" and the other, wisely, replied; "Too much of an anti-climax. Mustn't spoil a marvellous day. Let's go down for a pint." And we did, leaving the noisy, crowded snows to the mob.

It should be made clear that I do not write of cross-country skiing with narrow Nordic skis and lightweight boots since I have never tried this. I suspect that this equipment is not the most suitable for the steep or icy places regularly encountered in mountain skiing. Ski mountaineers dress like winter mountaineers – not like the gaily-bedecked whizz-kids you see in the advertisements or the racers on television – and carry rucksacks and, when necessary, ice axes. Nowadays, my tours are unambitious though still rewarding and memories of earlier, more challenging days, remain. Somehow, you never forget ski mountaineering days, whether in sunshine or in storm. The happy, crowded days of piste skiing in Lakeland, Scotland or the Alps have now all merged in a hazy, mixed-up picture of sun and spindrift, good turns and bad ones, superb swoops and ego-dashing falls, whereas I think I can recall, in some detail, all the dozens or scores of ski mountaineering days in their more natural environment, far from the crowds. A fortnight's successful Alpine hut-to-hut tour, some wonderful mountain rounds in Scotland and, in Lakeland, a fine circuit of the sunlit Kentmere Horseshoe in superb powder snow, are remembered with particular pleasure.

It has to be confessed, though, that my most recent skiing, with a daughter living in Vancouver, has been on the beautifully-laundered pistes of Cypress Bowl and Mount Whistler in British Columbia and Mount Baker in Washington, USA, where skins – and even rucksacks – seemed unknown, where nobody walked or climbed more than 10 yards, and where hired, fancy looking downhill boots were used instead of my heavy ski mountaineering footgear. It was all so easy – by car on cleared mountain highways to the foot of the lifts and then up and down one run after another on superb, piste snow, so flattering to one's style that I began to wonder, after all these years, whether perhaps even I could really ski. There were no queues or crowds – we avoided the weekends – the sun blazed down all day and, from the top of the lifts, we looked across at wave after wave of real mountains. At seventy-five years of age there is now the temptation to settle for this sort of thing – or might be if it was more readily available – but, back home, the sight from my windows of snow covered High Street, Harter Fell, Red Screes or the Howgills is still alluring and, now and again, and, indeed, as often as possible, I have, forgetting all the effort involved, got out on the tops. The skiing on these untracked snows may not be so neat and elegant as on the pistes – 'rough-neck skiing' is how Rusty Westmorland described it in his '*It's Tough but It's Grand*' in our 1948 *Journal* – although I can think of many splendid slopes in our fells that have provided perfect skiing. But, bagging winter summits in this way, you feel you have had a real mountaineering day.

Regrettably, to a would-be ski mountaineer, probably most members of the Lake District Ski Club are downhill fanatics – and some very good at it indeed. But we should commend the club for its energy and enterprise in hut building, tow construction, Scottish and Alpine meets and, now, ski racing and congratulate them on fifty years of mountain activity and much good fellowship. Skiing, whether on smoothed or untracked snow, is a wonderful outdoor exercise and for myself, as for many members of the Fell and Rock, there is always the recurring problem in winter – whether to climb, walk or ski. Leslie Somervell started off a lot of things when, in the early 1900s , inspired by Nansen's Greenland adventures, he made himself a pair of skis which were still in use by younger members of his family thirty years later. He had the right idea about mountains and skiing, and perhaps in its next half-century more and more members of the club he helped to found – and other skiers as well – will be encouraged to leave the crowded pistes and seek quieter, but even more rewarding, adventures on the heights.

PART FOUR

Mountains and Music

These random effusions, cobbled together in my dotage, have been written entirely for my own enjoyment. Not for money and certainly not for the ephemeral whiff of so-called fame. These geriatric musings are about things I love – mountains and music – and, as old Alf Wainwright used to say: "You don't expect to be paid for writing love letters".

So, when it's raining – as it was in Kendal during much of the time when I was knocking out the book – and I can't get out on the hills, very little hills, nowadays, it has been pleasant to sit at my word-processor, and, later, my laptop, and write a few paragraphs about things that to me at the time seemed particularly interesting or even slightly important. Little things, mainly, nothing exciting nor world shattering, but all about mountains and music, the most important things in my long life, apart from my family.

Mountains – and this includes rock climbing, snow and ice climbing, fell-walking, gill scrambling, skiing, the changing scenery, seasons and weather, sheep, red deer, golden eagles, stone walls, flowers, clouds, the magic of sunlight on snow, dawns, sunsets and a hundred and one other things – have been my whole life since boyhood and, deep down, have always seemed far more important to me than mundane things like a job or, say, a motorcar.

And since the age of six when I started my piano lessons – my parents were very far-sighted – music has always been almost as important as mountains. Indeed, my most valuable possession – far more valuable, to me, than my car, even if I was to buy a new Mercedes or Jaguar next week – is my old Challen upright piano which I bought new for £700 when I "retired" nearly thirty years ago.

After 87 years of practice, starting, unwillingly, at the age of six, I'm still trying to play the piano – with increasing difficulty in the last few years since I broke two fingers of my right hand in a slip on the ice in the Howgills. Right-hand chords, especially octaves, are now painful and difficult but the struggle is, I suppose, some sort of therapy. For the first two or three years after the accident I couldn't manage to play anything at all, but I've just struggled this morning through the piano score of Beethoven's B flat major piano concerto – very slowly and very badly. And now I'm going to try to play it every day for two or three weeks to see if I can approach my performances of, say, ten years ago – not very exciting though they were. The B flat is not my favourite Beethoven piano concerto: that would probably be the No 5, The Emperor, but they're all good. Beethoven had one of the most profound musical minds that ever existed – a man of tremendous imagination and awesome ability.

Incidentally, my favourite piano concertos are probably not any of the Beethovens, not even the Emperor, but perhaps Rachmaninoff Nos 2 and 3 – especially No 3 which is the most difficult piano concerto I know. I've been trying to play them both for many years, at one time practising every day, but there're just too many notes to crowd on to my crooked fingers and the result is, always, quite appalling. But, even today, I enjoy the struggle immensely, awful though the sound always is, and I suppose I'm not too bad, for my age, at the easier, slow movement of the No 2. Fortunately for all concerned nobody hears me play. I do it in splendid privacy.

Come to think of it, though, I did once play in public, in a sort of way. Once, in the 1990's, they came to do a television piece about me – the climbing, the books and the "Guardian" pieces. They crowded into my drawing-room – about a dozen of them with all their equipment – and the director noticed my piano. "Do you play?" he asked and when I said I did, a little, he decided they would have me playing background music for the film. He then announced they would go up the fellside at the back of the house, use a telephoto lens and "zoom" on to me, from behind, through the window, playing the piano. They all then trooped out of the house and up the fellside where they set up their equipment leaving behind just one man – the sound recordist.

He was a peculiar, little man with a pronounced Lancashire accent and, throughout the hour or two he was in my drawing-room, he kept his hat, a flat cap, firmly on his head. I decided to play the Beethoven that happened to be on the piano – the slow movement of the piano concerto in C minor, No 3 – and the sound recordist took up his position lying on the floor near the pedals of the piano with his sound equipment – a sort of woolly tube about a yard long.

I played my piece, trying to forget the funny, little man at my feet and quietly thought I had played it rather well – for me. So when he unravelled himself and his equipment from the floor I asked him: "How did that sound?" And Flat Cap answered firmly: "Too much bloody pedal" – my first, and only, music criticism. Eventually, the programme was shown on television and there I was playing the Beethoven in my untidy, old sweater with my hair uncombed. It certainly wasn't concert hall stuff but it didn't sound all that awful. Perhaps rather ponderous, I thought later. And that was my one and only public appearance – if you can call television a public appearance. But no, I remember now there was a second one for the programme was repeated a month or two later.

But, moving from the ridiculous to the sublime, I've seen and listened to Rachmaninoff playing all his concertos and also his wonderful Rhapsody on a Theme of Paganini and, once, not many years before his death in 1943 at the age of seventy, I had the great pleasure of interviewing him at the Free Trade Hall in Manchester, the then-home of the Hallé Orchestra. But Rachmaninoff was only one of the great musicians I've been privileged, as a journalist, to meet and, later on, I may tell you about some of them.

MUSICAL BEGINNINGS

Many years ago I was giving an "off the cuff" talk about music at my Rotary Club. Perhaps I was filling in for another speaker who hadn't turned up. So I just drooled on, without notes or any idea what I was going to say, about some of the great musicians I had had the great, good fortune, as a journalist, to meet. I'm sure it was painfully boring, for I was very cocky, over-confident and woefully immature in those days, but on I went about Sir Thomas Beecham, Galli-Curci, Paul Robeson, Paderewski, Rachmaninoff and several others, all of whom I'd interviewed or chatted with over the years. When I'd been droning on for about twenty minutes, one of the members, Leslie Powell, who happened to be a very knowledgeable musician and choirmaster – he was also the coroner – got up and, in a pained, little voice of near despair, asked: "Excuse me. Did you ever meet Beethoven?" And that, of course, was the end of my talk and the complete deflation of my ego. I crawled off the top table in shame.

Regrettably, I have no cuttings of newspaper reports of those early chats with some of the most important people in classical music at that time. If I had cuttings these hazy reminiscences would have been far easier to write. In some cases, I didn't write anything about the chat – not even about my talk with Rachmaninoff – since these were often done purely out of my own interest and not for the benefit of my paper. And, in the cases where I had been doing an actual interview, I never bothered to file a cutting in those days up to seventy years ago. I never even thought about keeping cuttings and, even today, being a very lazy and unorganised person, I very rarely preserve any cuttings – or reviews – of my writings although some pieces, including my Country Diary contributions to *The Guardian*, are filed away in my word processor. How much easier – but more complex – things would be today if we had had computers seventy years ago?

First, though, a few words about how I "discovered" music in the days before television, compact discs and concerts, when even radio was in its infancy. You couldn't say I came from a musical family. None of my relations could play any instrument, although I believe my father had once tinkered with the euphonium, and so far as I know, none of them ever went to a concert. But, to my great, good fortune, my father and my three uncles were all fond of church music and were competent singers. And one or two of them, at least, could sight-sing – not very well, but good enough.

The ability to sight-sing – to sing a completely unknown piece of music from the score and to hold on to, say, the bass line or the tenor, when the man next to you is singing something completely different, is a tremendous gift. Even today, I would happily give the price of a new car to be able to do it properly.

Bored with working on maths, Latin or French verbs I turned to the piano for solace and encouragement and first, rather strangely, "discovered" Grieg's piano pieces, perhaps moving on to Beethoven later. How well I recall my cousin Edwin, of about my own age, telling me about first hearing Beethoven's fifth symphony – "absolutely fantastic" he said. I think we then listened together to a squeaky old record of it played on an ancient gramophone and both agreed this was the greatest music we'd ever heard. I don't know if there was any "pop" music in those days but if there was we weren't interested in it – and never have been. And that was really the beginning of my musical education. The years of piano lessons beforehand had all been wasted for my ears had never been opened to proper music but merely to simple tunes of little merit. Nobody had spurred me to enjoy good music nor had even talked to me about it. I suppose I really "discovered" music for myself – after my early enjoyment of hymns and "Messiah" around the piano.

My first encounters with some of the great musicians of the day came in the early 1930s when I was working on a

Lancashire evening paper. Occasional series of "celebrity" concerts were being staged in Preston at that time and I persuaded my editor to let me have a shot at interviewing the celebrities – mostly in the Park Hotel near the railway station where they were accommodated, in some luxury, I seem to remember. And one of the first of them to fall into my clutches was the giant singer, Paul Robeson, then at the height of his powers and fame.

Talking to Robeson in his pleasant hotel bedroom I realised what a huge man he was. His hands, which I grasped at the beginning and end of our talk, were the largest I had ever seen – about four times bigger than my own. Hands that could pick up a rugger ball or, I would think, half a cow, with ease. But Robeson seemed the kindliest of men and put up with my, probably, fatuous questioning with gentle, good humour. Indeed, I have nearly always found that the greater the man the more patient, gentle and understanding he has appeared in conversation. It has always been the lesser men who have been difficult.

My principal memory of Robeson – apart from the size of his hands – was our discussion on quarter-tones. I told him I knew about half-tones – going from fah to fee, for example – but how on earth could you sing something in between? So, Robeson sang some quarter-tones for me in his bedroom, as we sat together on the bed, showing that it could be done, and then told me how the natives of the Outer Hebrides sang in quarter-tones in their wistful, impressive singing of almost long-forgotten ancient Highland airs.

So, here was this huge, kindly American singer, sitting with me on his bed, telling me all about the songs of the Outer Isles. I thought I would have known about this part of the world far better than he, already being an ardent explorer, as a mountaineer, of Scotland and the western isles, but Robeson, surprisingly, seemed to know all these lovely, out-of-the-way places and a great deal about their music. We must have chatted for at least an hour on a score of topics and I left with my head buzzing with the deep, deep music of this lovely man. All this happened about seventy years ago but the picture and the sounds are still clearly with me today.

THE GREAT TOMMY BEECHAM

The most ebullient "character" among all the great conductors, pianists, violinists and singers I've had the good fortune to meet was, undoubtedly, Sir Thomas Beecham, Bart. He was a man of tremendous ability and enthusiasms – and always crying out to be noticed. And, yet, the first time we met, he passed completely unnoticed by hundreds, possibly, thousands of people. I had arranged to meet him at the Park Hotel, Preston, and walk with him to the Public Hall, where he was to conduct a "celebrity" concert that evening. I don't think Sir Thomas had been to Preston before: at least, he'd no idea where the Public Hall was.

So there we were – this dapper, little man with his trim goatee beard, probably the best-known musical figure in Europe at that time, and myself walking up Fishergate through the crowds of shoppers and sightseers – and nobody spotted him. We were both talking animatedly – even loudly, in his case – with Sir Thomas stopping now and then to emphasise a point, but I could have been walking up the street with a colleague from the office for all the attention that was paid to us. I had expected that we would have been stopped every few yards by people saying: "Excuse me, are you Sir Thomas Beecham?" But no, the best known face in music, at that time, escaped recognition in Preston that day in the 1930s. I think he himself was, privately, surprised, and, perhaps, even disappointed, for he was the complete showman.

His entrance on to the platform at any concert was always dramatic. First of all, he would wait for a minute or two to heighten the tension and then walk purposefully, with neat, little strides to the conductor's desk. A tap with his stick and an emphatic downbeat and the concert would begin. Sometimes he could be heard humming the tune as the music poured out and, almost always, in an appropriate moment, there would be a joke or a witticism.

For Sir Thomas had an extremely quick brain, was completely self-possessed and had the wonderful gift of always being able to cap a situation with a funny and appropriate remark. Dozens of stories illustrate his witticisms, one or two of which I heard him perpetrate at the time. This one is a favourite. He was rehearsing a major work and the orchestra had gone several minutes into the piece when a man – I think he was a second trombone – was seen crawling, rather clumsily, to his seat on the back row of the brass. No doubt, he'd been too long in the bar. Immediately, banging his baton on the desk, Sir Thomas stopped the music and addressed the orchestra.

"You, there, the man who's just crawled in! Stand up!" And the man, visibly terrified by the dressing-down he expected, stood up. "What's your name?" demanded Sir Thomas and the man replied in a squeaky, tremulous voice: "Ball, sir". To which Tommy, with a flicker of a smile, languidly replied, quick as a flash: "How singular!" I thought this quite brilliant.

There was the story, too, about his feeling for some modern composers. He was asked whether he had ever played the music of Stockhausen, John Cage or some other "difficult" modern composer to which Sir Thomas replied: 'No, but I've trodden in some!"

We met several times over the years, Sir Thomas and I, and I came to know him fairly well. On one occasion, before the war, I went to see him at his suite in the Midland Hotel, Manchester to ask him about the programme for a forthcoming "celebrity concert" in either Preston or Manchester. Having been directed to his private suite I knocked on a door and walked in. And there, disporting himself in his bath, was the great Sir Thomas. I had gone through the wrong door.

I must say he took the intrusion very well. Instead of cursing me for my stupidity and throwing me out of the bathroom he carefully pulled on a bathrobe, and then some slippers, and ushered me out to his drawing room. I especially remember the slippers. They looked Turkish, or, at least, oriental, with the toes curled up like the front of a gondola.

Once seated in his pleasant drawing room he spoke on the phone to some manager or official to enquire about the programme and then started to tell me about it. But, before he had got very far, he said, to my amazement: "Tell you what! Why don't you tell me what we should play?"

As quickly as I could pull myself together I starred to blurt out some suggestions – an overture, I think it was Mendelssohn's "Midsummer Night's Dream", perhaps a Schubert or Beethoven symphony, and then a final, fairly energetic piece. And, with quiet authority, Sir Thomas immediately picked up the phone again to check with his manager or orchestra librarian whether or not they had all the scores of these pieces available. Then he turned to me again, told me he didn't think much of my suggested last piece, and added: "No. We'll finish off with Francesca da Rimini. It's a bloody good row!" And that was the programme they played – my suggested pieces with all the excitement and colour of the Tchaikovsky to finish off.

I wish I'd been able to spend more time with Sir Thomas, although, in several meetings, I must have had more than a few hours of his time. I admired him tremendously – for his musical ability, his confidence, his self-possession, his way with an audience and his ready wit. I wish I'd had the chance to hear his views on some of the great composers but we were too many generations apart – me, at the beginning of my musical life, he, towards the end of his. But I'm so grateful for the time he gave to me – an unknown, gauche interviewer. Certainly, he was one of the musical personalities of the century – a showman but a gentleman. They said he was a musical "amateur" – not professionally trained – but he had more music in his heart than many professors and doctors of music and he introduced millions to its delights.

REMEMBERING RACHMANINOFF

As a young man all I knew about Rachmaninoff was that he had written the famous Prelude in C Sharp Minor which everybody who played the piano or listened to piano music knew. Indeed, I used to play, or try to play, this famous prelude, with its crashing chords and surging rhythms, myself – probably very badly indeed – for it was a powerful piece and you could really let yourself go on it. To an impressionable youth it seemed to describe the never-ending struggles of a man trapped in a coffin or tomb, and desperately trying, without success, to claw his way out. Rachmaninoff, to me then, was just a composer who could write exciting pieces. I didn't know whether he was still alive but probably assumed he must be long dead, like most of the others. His name seemed to be spelled either with "off" or "ov" at the end but I'm using "off" here because I assume this is the anglicised form of the Russian "ov". And it was spelled this way – Rachmaninoff – in the programme for his memorial concert at the Royal Albert Hall in London on June 7th, 1943 which I was fortunate enough to attend – just before I was shipped off to the 14th Army in Burma to fight the Japanese.

But, long before then, in, I think, about 1937, I heard, for the first time, his wonderful second piano concerto which affected me almost as much as my "discovery" of Beethoven as a teenager. I was working at the time in Manchester on the *Daily Mail* – then a serious broadsheet, rather like the *Telegraph* today – and I think I heard the concerto at an afternoon concert – not at the Hallé's Free Trade Hall but at some smaller concert hall on, I think, Deansgate. This, I thought, was tremendously exciting music and I wanted to hear more of it, especially his other piano concertos, and also discover something about the composer himself.

Rachmaninoff's second piano concerto in C minor is probably the best-loved piano concerto in the world. The only other one that may come close to it in popular esteem is Tchaikovsky's No 1. The Rachmaninoff No 2 has wonderful tender or passionate themes and a really exciting solo part. Years after I first heard it the concerto was extensively used by the director, David Lean, in the famous film, "Brief Encounter" which was partly filmed in Carnforth railway station, twenty-odd miles south of my home. And the Rachmaninoff No 2 has regularly been voted, by listeners, the No 1 piece of music in Classic FMs "Best One Hundred" tunes.

Remarkably, I was able to meet the composer not long after first hearing the No 2 – either in late 1937 or in 1938. By this time I was attending all the concerts given by the Hallé Orchestra at the Free Trade Hall in Manchester as a so-called music critic. Most of these concerts were conducted by Sir Thomas Beecham but, in several cases, Malcolm Sargent, or some other conductor, was in charge and the soloists sometimes included great pianists like Schnabel or violinists like Kreisler, Ida Haendel or Huberman.

Then, one evening, Rachmaninoff was the solo pianist playing his third piano concerto – the most difficult of all – and his wonderful Rhapsody on a Theme of Paganini. At the end of the concert, exhilarated by the music, I asked if I could speak to the great man and, since I was representing the *Daily Mail*, then a prestigious newspaper, I was given every facility and conducted to his dressing room.

Incredibly, I took no notes and wrote nothing about the interview – or, rather, chat which is what it really was. My job, as Northern Music Critic of the *Daily Mail*, was merely to write two or three hundred words about the concert and I had to hurry away to my telephone in Deansgate to catch the edition so the interview, if you could call it that, was rather short.

Sergei Vassilyevitch Rachmaninoff was then about 64 years of age – he died, at his home in Beverley Hills, California, five or six years later, in March 1943.He was quite a tall man and he carried himself very well, like a soldier. Indeed, he looked exactly how I imagined a Prussian officer looked, although he had never been in the army, hair cropped very close on a bullet-shaped head. He also looked very melancholy and sad, with pouches under his eyes, and gave the impression that he rarely smiled, that life was pretty grim.

But, mostly, I looked at his hands – the hands of probably the greatest pianist in the world at that time – and was surprised they looked almost podgy and not the elegant and athletic hands that churned out those tremendous, complicated chords and intricate runs. I have read somewhere that Rachmaninoff was supposed to have the largest hands of any musician and that that was why he could encompass those difficult stretches but they didn't look all that big to me. Perhaps about half the size of Paul Robeson's, I thought. But they could certainly tackle complex music probably better than any other pianist at that time.

We chatted easily about the music – I don't think, being young, I was especially overawed by the great man – and he answered all my inane questions very pleasantly and courteously, although he must have realised that I was really out of my depth. But then, some devil inside me prompted me to ask him the most cheeky, impertinent and meaningless question I could have put to him. Did he not think, I could hear myself unbelievably saying, that he had played the No 3 perhaps a little too quickly? Would it not have sounded better if it had been played just a little slower? Sixty-five years after that conversation that has, fortunately, never been reported anywhere I can only recall that the great man's reply to this impertinence was wise and gentle and that he clearly forgave me my reckless behaviour. Obviously, the man who had composed the work was the person most qualified to decide on its speed but the mournful, lugubrious Rachmaninoff was also kind and forgiving. Thank you, Sergei, for your kindly tolerance of a very gauche interviewer all those years ago. Strangely, I have a treasured compact disc of Rachmaninoff playing his No 3 in, I think, America, and he does seem to take it at a tremendous speed – much faster than the rate at which it is played by other pianists. So this is how it should be played.

A MEDLEY OF MUSICIANS

Apart from Paul Robeson and one or two others I have few memories of talks or interviews with singers before the war: I was more interested, at that time, in instrumentalists – especially pianists – and conductors. But, among my early victims when I was talking with "celebrity concert" personalities in the luxury Park Hotel, Preston was the famous diva, Galli-Curci-Amelita. Galli-Curci, born in Milan in 1882 was said to be, or have been, "the greatest coloratura soprano in the world". I must have spent at least half an hour chatting to her in her sumptuous apartment. I don't remember writing anything about her but I still have a vague notion that she was rather short and had black hair.

I can do a little better with John McCormack, the great Irish tenor, often billed as Count John McCormack – a Papal order, I think – for at least he sang for me. We met, as usual, in the splendid Park Hotel and spent a good hour talking to each other. I think I probably asked him if he would kindly sing for me – I was very cheeky, in those days – and he obliged, in the privacy of his bedroom, by singing "The garden where the praties grow" in a wonderful soaring, rather high-pitched, tenor voice. He was a big, well-built man and an impressive sight when in full flow. And Count John McCormack – at that time, some years before World War II – was perhaps the outstanding tenor in the world, always performing to sold-out houses. Indeed, at one time, it was said, his record royalties exceeded even those of the great Enrico Caruso. John McCormack was chiefly remarkable for his breath control and, especially, for his famous pianissimo at the close of his songs.

A third great singer whom I met on two or three occasions was the charming Austrian, Richard Tauber. Initially, he had been an opera singer, first with the Dresden Opera and later with the Vienna Staatsoper, and sang on most of the world's great opera stages. Then, for about ten years, in collaboration with Franz Lehar, he became famous as an operetta singer, and he was also a composer and conductor. However, Tauber's father was half-Jewish and Richard ran foul of the Nazis and had to flee Hitler's Germany and, later, Austria. Britain, though, welcomed him and Tauber settled in England, continued to sing in opera and operetta, gave scores of concerts, made hundreds of recordings and even appeared in films – once, as Schubert.

I first heard Tauber sing at a "celebrity concert" in Preston in either 1936 or 1937 and later met him, informally, in both Manchester and London. His wife was an attractive actress and at parties after a concert or show Tauber would sport a monocle – not, I believe, for affectation but out of necessity. For me, Tauber was at his best singing Schubert lieder and I can imagine, and almost hear him now, as I write, declaiming "Dein ist mein Herz" ("Thine is my Heart") in "Impatience" ("Ungeduld"), one of the most famous of Schubert's songs. Tauber died, from cancer, in 1948 – singing right up to the end. He was only 57 at his death. I remember him as a friendly, companionable man with a wonderful voice – easy, sociable, rather chubby, with a twinkle in his eye.

Hidden away in a dusty drawer in a desk near my piano is my little treasure trove – a big pile of programmes of the Hallé Concerts Society starting in the 1937 season and continuing to the start of World War II – all the concerts I attended in Manchester as a so-called music critic. And with them is another pile of programmes of "International Celebrity concerts", starting in 1936 – all of them full of memories of musical evenings up to seventy years ago. Glancing quickly through them I see many famous names – at least they were famous in those far-off days, and most are still fondly remembered. They include pianists such' as Schnabel, Paderewski and Edwin Fischer, violinists like Kreisler, Ida Haendel or Huberman and singers including the great Beniamino Gigli, singing "Celeste Aida" and, from Tosca, "The stars are brightly shining".

The two principal conductors at these dozens of concerts were Sir Thomas Beecham – I'd met him several times by then – and the popular Malcolm Sargent – not knighted at this time and usually known as Dr Malcolm Sargent. Strangely, for I attended many of his concerts, I never had the pleasure of meeting this fine maestro. He was especially noted for his inspired conducting of the great choral works and I particularly remember his "Messiah", Haydn's "The Creation" and Elgar's "The Dream of Gerontius".

Principal singers in these works often included Isabel Baillie and Heddle Nash. I met Isabel Baillie on several occasions and remember once having a meal with her and one or two others in the main hotel in Morecambe, of all places – she must have been singing at a concert in the area – when she discovered a beetle or some sort of creepie-crawlie in her soup. Instead of making a scene which might have been expected from some prima donnas she quietly asked for the head waiter, showed him her plate and requested another meal. I was most impressed by her quiet but determined demeanour.

Another concert I particularly remember at the Hallé's

headquarters in Manchester, the Free Trade Hall, was the visit of the Prague Philharmonic Orchestra with Rafael Kubelik conducting. They played, among other things, Dvorak's wonderful "From the New World" symphony and also the tuneful Vltava from Smetana's "Ma Vlast". After the concert I met Kubelik and had a few words with him but I mostly recall his exhuberant conducting – almost dancing on his toes, at times, and exhorting, say, the trumpets or the French horns, so that they rose to their feet all together, playing their instruments – rather like a "pop" orchestra, I'm sorry to say. I'd not seen this sort of thing at a classical concert before, nor since, and can't say I enjoyed it but the music was wonderful.

Nearly all these old Hallé concert programmes – many of them defaced by my shorthand notes for the piece I was having to telephone immediately the concert had finished – included several bars of the main melodies in the symphony or concerto. And these I would play on the piano at my "digs" or when I got home – I married in September 1937 and lived in, first, Didsbury and then Chorlton-cum-Hardy – so that I could recall the big tunes at the concert. Indeed, I played several of these mini-scores just before I knocked out these lines on my laptop – a pleasant reminder of some of the great music that has inspired me throughout most of my long life. Glancing through these old programmes it is interesting to note the amount of Delius the Hallé used to play – he was a particular favourite of Sir Thomas Beecham – and remember the visits, as conductors, of Felix Weingartner or Eugene Goossens or, as solo violinist, of Henry Holst, son of Gustav Holst, composer of "The Planets".

One thing I particularly regretted during these interesting Hallé pre-war years was that I never had the opportunity to meet Sir John Barbarolli nor even to watch him conducting – except on television. For, not long after the war broke out, I impetuously and probably inadvisedly, volunteered for military service, long before my age group came up, and eventually found myself in Burma in the "Forgotten" 14th Army. But all that's another story and nothing to do with either mountains or music.

Bert Smith of Coniston, though, had a great deal to do with music – in the same way that Stradivari had. For his job was making violins and he had only one relaxation from his demanding, dedicated craft – he also enjoyed playing them. So Bert Smith rightly comes into my Medley of Musicians chapter for he was just as much a musician as Kreisler – if not even more so for he was a craftsman, as well as a performer.

I think he died in the early 1970s but, before then, I had met him several times and came to know him quite well. He lived in a terrace house in Coniston and worked mostly in an attic. Through a tiny roof window he could see a line of crags and, above them, the sky, but Bert had no time to look at the scenery for he had much work to do. He was up at six o'clock every morning, summer and winter, weekdays and Sundays, and never put down his tools until ten o'clock at night. He lived for his job and his job was making violins that were as good, or better, than any others. And many distinguished violinists – Albert Sammons was one – believed they were.

For Bert Smith's violins were, all of them, exact copies of the great Italian master craftsmen such as Stradivari and Guarneri, with the curves carved, not bent. You can buy violins made in a factory, the wood bent by steam, but Bert Smith didn't like machinery. Everything had to be made by hand. Even his tools he had made himself. Every year he made four violins, fashioning each part, except the strings, with his own hands. Once when I called on him – probably on my way back to the car after a visit to Dow Crag – he played for me on the violin he was completing. I do remember the tone he was producing out of this smooth piece of wood at which he had been chipping away for months was, really, out of this world.

"How do you get this wonderful tone?" was my obvious question. And his answer was equally obvious. "That's my secret." But he was prepared to tell me part of the story. Most of the secret, it seemed, was in the varnishing –at least a six months job – and the rest was in the tuning of the back of the violin. For hours at a time, day after day, this little man was tapping away at his thin pieces of wood, listening to the sound, taking off a shaving, and listening again – until he got exactly the sound he wanted. Only then would he be satisfied – and begin work on his next violin.

I never knew the price of a Bert Smith violin – not as much as a Stradivari, of course – but they weren't cheap for Bert Smith was both a master craftsman and a fine violinist. And his violins were not made in a foreign factory by machinery but in the attic of a terrace house in the middle of the Lake District by hand and had each taken months of patient work to produce. People who own a Bert Smith, just like people who own a Strad – and there must be many of them scattered about the country – should be immensely proud of their genuine handmade violin. It'll be worth a fortune – or should be.

MUSIC OF THE GODS

I'm quite sure that Beethoven must have been one of the biggest influences in my life and, always, an inspiration never to give in. His music seems to have a majestic grandeur not equalled by other composers. Clearly he thought and felt more deeply than his predecessors. Beethoven was the very first composer I discovered and he is the composer that I've studied in far greater detail than any other. One reason for this is that, many years ago, I acquired – it might have been from an Oxfam or similar shop – a superb (by Schirmer of New York) compilation of Beethoven's symphonies arranged, for four hands, on the piano. Two of you, seated together, could play a symphony, one, on the right, playing the main theme with two hands, the other, on the left, playing the bass. My daughter, Sandra, and I often used to play together, in this way, sometimes producing almost a resemblance – in the easier passages – to the actual music. The delightful allegretto in his wonderful seventh symphony – especially the measured tread in the bass – was one of our favourites and also much of the easier sections of the sixth ("Pastoral") symphony.

This wonderful compilation was in two volumes but I only managed to acquire the second one which consists of symphonies numbers six to nine – the tremendous "Choral" symphony. Many people would agree that – apart from the fifth, which I had in another book and the majestic third (the "Eroica") which I was always playing on compact disc – these are his very greatest symphonies. I played them on my own on the piano – mostly the main theme, with two hands – for years and years, sometimes every day, so that I could fairly claim to know every note of these four symphonies. Strange that his even-numbered symphonies have less punch and are not nearly so adventurous as the odd-numbered symphonies which are far more profound and challenging – and among the finest symphonies ever written. In addition I practised his five piano concertos, including the great "Emperor", on my piano for many years and also a great deal of his other work – especially his piano sonatas, including the "Moonlight" which I must have played scores of times. You could almost say I was steeped in Beethoven.

But, although Beethoven was pre-eminent, in my view, among composers for the majestic breadth of his music – and still is – there was another composer whose works, or some of them, moved me even more for their beauty and serene, almost tragic, melancholy. This was Schubert. Very many years ago I had to give a talk to some organisation or another – perhaps about the Lake District – and, at the end, the chairman, without any warning, asked me what piece of music I would chose were I to be abandoned on a desert island. And, without thinking, right off the top of my head, I said: "Schubert's string quintet in C". It was a completely spontaneous reaction. I'd never considered the matter before but this work must have moved me, perhaps years earlier, more than any other. This was one of Schubert's very last works, written just before his death in 1828 and the wonderful second movement, the Adagio, can really tear at your heart strings with inexpressible sadness. Very little of Schubert's music was heard or published during his lifetime and five of his nine symphonies were only unearthed thirty years after his death – by the young Arthur Sullivan and George Grove of Grove's Dictionary. The so-called "Unfinished" symphony, the 8th in B minor, is a most popular work but the "Great" C major symphony, one of his last compositions, is, by far, his finest symphonic achievement, the rhythms washing in waves over you as you listen, spellbound, to the changing melodies.

Indeed, it is Schubert's latest works, written as he was approaching death – he died at the early age of 31 – that express the real genius and musical poetry of the man. These include the "Great" C major symphony, the string quintet in C, some of the great string quartets, including the tragic "Death and the Maiden", the wonderful late piano trios and the superb B flat sonata that I have been trying to play on my piano for as long as I can remember. The slow movement of this sonata is one of the most heart-rending pieces of music I know. In addition to all this, Schubert, who must have written more melodies than anybody else in the history of music, wrote up to six hundred songs – the musical settings of dozens of poets – including the mighty "Erlkonig" written when he was only eighteen, and the song cycles of Die Winterreise, Die Schone Mullerin and his swansong, Schwanengesang. Naturally, Schubert worshipped Beethoven and asked to be buried as near to him as possible. He was a torch bearer at Beethoven's funeral – just two years before his own. So passed, two years apart, two of the greatest musical geniuses in history – the Titan wrestling with the gods and the outstanding singing poet of music.

And there I really must end the chapter, without even mentioning Verdi, Haydn and hundreds of others – just a small selection of a few great composers who have moved and inspired me and taught me so much about life. All of it music of the gods without which life would have been bleak indeed. This is why my piano is still my most valued possession and why great tunes, running through my mind, have often got me up many climbs and mountains.

GREAT MOMENTS IN THE HILLS

Most of the time we're in the hills we're happy – except when we're wet through, frozen, lost, frightened, injured or in the wrong valley with night coming on – but there are also moments, or even minutes or longer, that can be said to have made our day. Moments that made everything seem worth while. Moments we would remember for years. Great moments in the hills.

Climbers especially remember the great joy of a first ascent or the completion of a particularly severe pitch and there is always a great sense of relief and utter satisfaction – ecstasy even – when, leading a hard snow and ice route in winter, we pull out over the cornice. In many cases, perhaps in most, we climb out of the dark shadows, for winter gullies are usually on north faces, often into sunlight glinting on the snow. A completely new world.

The first time you led a "very severe" – in my early climbing days, more than seventy years ago, this was the highest grade – was always a great moment. Nowadays, with all their gear, youngsters seem to get on to very severes, about half-way through the grades, after they've been climbing a week or two. How well I remember leading my first VS in about 1930 or it could have been 1929. It was Eagle's Nest Ridge Direct on Great Gable, first climbed by Godfrey A. Solly on a cold April day in 1892 – one of the outstanding feats in early Lake District climbing history. The second man on this redoubtable climb – almost literally steadying the leader's feet on the steep, exposed main pitch – was the famous W. C. Slingsby, revered in Norway as their legendary mountain pioneer and the father-in-law of Geoffrey Winthrop Young, climber and mountain poet.

I had met Solly at Wasdale Head – a very old man with a white beard but still climbing in the 1930s – and, years later, I met both Geoffrey Winthrop Young and Slingsby's daughter Eleanor, usually known as Len, on several occasions. To Solly was often ascribed the instruction: "Silence whilst the leader is advancing". He had the gravitas and demeanour for such a remark but he was, nevertheless, a very remarkable mountaineer – a Grand Old Man of the crags. In the early 1930s I had watched Winthrop Young climbing on Dow Crag with George Bower leading and a third man helping to put Geoffrey's peg leg on to the holds.

Whether or not Eagle's Nest Ridge Direct is still regarded as a VS I'm not sure. In a later guide I notice it was down-graded to VS-mild. But when Solly led it it was regarded as the hardest climb in the country: very steep and exposed, on a cold day and climbed in clumsy, nailed boots. But I led it wearing rubber plimsolls on a warm, summer's day and I had as my second my early climbing mentor, George Basterfield, one of the best climbers in the country and – although I didn't know this at the time – the then-President of the Fell and Rock Climbing Club. Although I had then climbed, usually leading, several of the Napes ridges on Gable I had not tried Eagle's Nest, thinking it beyond my powers.

But George, bless him, thought otherwise and so off we went with me in the lead and George, behind me, quietly giving me advice – and encouragement. "Just step up quietly. Don't pull. There's nothing to it" I heard, floating up the rope – and there wasn't. Lower down he had advised me how to deal with the Parallel Cracks and, on the exposed ridge, there seemed no problem – with the best possible second behind me. How much more intimidating must have been that first ascent of Solly and Slingsby more than a hundred years ago. So this first VS of mine was certainly one of my great moments in the hills – several moments, I suppose, although I remember we fairly rattled up, being in good form in ideal conditions.

There's no doubt in my mind about my greatest day in British mountains – and I can't think of a day in the Alps or the Rockies or in the foothills of the Himalayas that I enjoyed more than this outing in, I think, 1957. This was the day I took my son, Robin, along the traverse of the Cuillin ridge in Skye. We were told afterwards it was probably the first father and son traverse, up to that time, and that Robin, who was 18, was possibly the youngest person, then, to have done the ridge. Since then, no doubt, many much younger teenagers may have done it and even granddads may have taken their grandchildren along, for all I know.

Skye was a much quieter place in the 1950s than it is today and the ridge, in those days, was not traversed all that often. It was still regarded as quite an achievement. Throughout the whole of that glorious September day we saw only one other person from leaving Glenbrittle, where we were staying, to our arrival at the Sligachan Inn. You couldn't hope for that quietude today.

We left the Lodge at Glen Brittle after dinner one evening and walked round the coast to the foot of the Gars-bheinn screes where we pitched a tent and managed about an hour's sleep before our ancient alarm went off at 3.30am. Then we set off, in the darkness, up the seemingly non-ending scree slope, each of us carrying two or three, cheap, disposable torches which just about got us to the summit. This ascent, in complete darkness, slipping and sliding on the screes, was, by far, the most trying part of the day. We had another nineteen summits, including thirty one separate pinnacles and tops, to climb but, having got this first one in the bag, we felt sure – although completely exhausted by the effort – that we were going to make it.

The first of many great moments that day came as we reached the summit and could just see the shadowy forms of the mountains around us and, far below, the vague shapes of islands afloat in a grey sea. It was not yet dawn but light enough to see what we were doing so we set off, at the trot, along the ridge. We didn't want to waste any time. I carried the rope – a heavy 120 foot length, far longer than we needed, but the only rope I had – the map and the compass. Robin carried everything else – the spare clothing, the food, the water, the slings, the Kendal Mint Cake and the raisins. Curiously, we ate very little food during the traverse, apart from the raisins, leaving much of it on the ridge for the birds. All we really wanted was water and raisins. We had earlier cached water on the ridge in two places and Robin had a third bottle in his rucksack. Regrettably, this burst, soaking all the contents, and depriving us of our main need but we coped somehow. And we had straws, for sipping from tiny pools on the rocks, if need be.

Dawn came, I remember, at ten minutes to seven and this was the main magical moment of the day. The finest of many great moments on the ridge. By this time we had gone a mile or two along the traverse, noticing, all the time, the lightening of the sky to the east. Then, all at once, the sun that must have been slowly creeping up behind the distant peak of Blaven, flooded the grey, misty landscape with new sparkling light and dancing shadows. A new day had dawned and it was magical. Now we could clearly see the whole line of the Outer Hebrides, far out on the horizon, like great ships riding at anchor and the bold line of the ridge stretching ahead with all the peaks and towers glowing in the sunlight. The craggy ridge ahead, a helter-skelter of rock peaks, didn't seem menacing but, in the unbroken sunshine and under cloudless, blue skies, friendly and welcoming. Smiling on our endeavour. We were going to do it – easily. This was the greatest moment that day.

Other great moments were the rock climbs which all went surprisingly easily in the superb, sunny, windless conditions – the abseil into the Thearlaich-Dubh gap, the climb up the other side which we did unroped, the Inaccessible Pinnacle, the triple summits of Bidean Druim nan Ramh and the Bhasteir Tooth. We had done them all before – Naismith's Route on the Tooth only two days before when it was greasy and awkward – but, despite all our reconnaissance, it was around the Tooth that we got off route for a while and wasted time. We took less than twelve hours for the Ridge but we would have put in quite a fast time if my route finding had been better.

No doubt our arrival in the afternoon on the last summit, Sgurr nan Gillean, was a great moment but, again, I ruined things by deciding to descend by the Western Ridge, our route of ascent – twice crossing the Gendarme, which fell down many years ago – instead of by the rather dreary tourist route, thinking this would save time. In fact, it turned out to be, after the ascent of the Gars-bheinn screes in the darkness, the most tiring part of the whole trip and probably the start of the gradual deterioration of my feet and toes.

I wrote earlier that we saw only one person that wonderful day. As I was arranging the rope for the abseil down the short side of the Inaccessible Pinnacle I saw a man sitting on top of Sgurr Dearg just below me – it was still early in the morning – and, to my great surprise he addressed me by name. I could then see he was John Jackson, then director of the Plas y Brenin mountain centre in North Wales, who had been a member of the successful British expedition to Kangchenjunga a few years earlier. Hearing we were doing the ridge – how, I couldn't imagine for we had tried to keep it quiet – he had got up early and climbed the mountain to see if we needed any help. And, without more ado, he grabbed our rope and rucksacks and set off, at great speed over the several summits of Sgurr na Banachdich, as we lazily trudged behind. John then left but took some of our unnecessary clothing down to the Lodge, leaving two bottles of beer there for us and informing Mollie that we were at least an hour ahead of schedule – all of it a very kindly gesture indeed.

Other nights in the mountains have often provided great moments and I especially recall two of them. The first of these happened when my brother Leslie and I were teenagers and had decided to see the dawn from Scafell Pike. We left our tent near Boot in Eskdale, climbed the mountain to a pile of rocks just below the summit ridge and tried to catch some sleep there. On waking at dawn we went up to the summit and saw the most extraordinary view. Not only could we see the Scottish hills very clearly – even the Highlands beyond the Lowland hills – but also Ireland, quite unmistakeable, far beyond the familiar sight of the Isle of Man. And not only this but when we walked a hundred yards or so to the south we could also pick out the Welsh mountains—England, Scotland, Ireland and Wales from the top of Scafell Pike, although not all of them from exactly the same place. Undoubtedly, the view of a lifetime and a very great moment in the hills.

The other great moment was dawn from the top of Helvellyn after a traverse of Striding Edge in the moonlight. I was going to bed one night many years ago when I was informed by telephone that it was a superb moonlight night, that I was wasting it by lying in bed and should be enjoying it on the tops. "I'll see you at your garden gate in half an hour" said my caller. "Get your sleeping bag". My caller was Graham MacPhee, a famous pioneer climber, especially of Ben Nevis, who, at that time was living only a few miles away from me.

So we drove to Grisedale and went up Helvellyn by way of Striding Edge in the moonlight, feeling like pygmies in a lunar landscape but making sure we went over all the little towers. Graham was a stickler for doing things right. I remember as we were walking along the Edge we could see its shadow projected across the far side of Red Tarn and almost imagine we could pick out our own shadows creeping along. At the summit we dozed in our sleeping bags for about an hour when we noticed the orange glow in the sky growing steadily brighter. It was just ten to five when the dawn came – the flaming tip of a fiery sun just lifting over the Northern Pennines. We watched the golden ball soar into the sky, felt its first rays, and then trotted down Swirral Edge for breakfast, feeling we had stolen an extra day. Certainly a great moment in the hills.

Sighting the Brocken Spectre, the greatly magnified shadow of the observer being thrown on to the mist by sunlight, is always a great moment in the hills. I've seen at least half a dozen of these, including two in Scotland, but the best one, by far, was on a snowbound winter's day on Wetherlam many years ago. Ted Stacey and I were intent on a snow climb on the east face of Wetherlam but found the whole area completely shrouded in fog. We had intended crossing the face on a rising diagonal line just below the main crag but, in the thick fog, couldn't see a thing or where to go.

So we did something I've never done before on a snow climb. We got out the compass, plotted a line to hit Wetherlam Edge just below the summit and set off with our axes and crampons. And, miraculously, we reached the ridge where we had hoped to arrive and carried on up the steepening snow towards the unseen summit and the first great moment. For, in one stride, we climbed out of the fog to see the whole of the Lake District, below us, completely covered in white cotton wool, sparkling in the sunlight, with the rocky summits of the Scafells, seven miles away across the sea of fog, sticking up above the eiderdown blanket like islands, and looking within throwing distance.

We basked for a while in the sunshine, marvelling at the scene, and then turned round to climb back down through the fog and, immediately, had our second great moment. For, apparently straddling a rock ridge, perhaps two hundred yards away, was a perfect Brocken Spectre with, not one but two, concentric rainbows – a double "glory", the only time I have seen one of these. I moved my arms, the Spectre moved his, and I marvelled again about the wonders of nature. And so we climbed down through the impenetrable fog which continued all the way down the mountainside and also on the roads as we drove back home. For a glorious few minutes we had been above the dark, damp, dreary fog enveloping the Lake District in a private, sunlit world of our own.

No doubt I could go on, for many chapters, detailing great moments like these that have added such brilliance to many, many hundreds of days in the hills but, on reflection, one of the great moments that most of us have seen many times is so simple and yet so dramatic that I think I should end the chapter with this picture. We are walking through the mountains in thick mist, perhaps using a compass or treading a familiar track, when, suddenly, a change in the wind, and the mist and cloud are torn away in a trice and the dale leaps up at you from far below your feet. This is a really great moment in the hills that all walkers have seen. To be treasured when our mountain days are over.

JOSIE'S HILLS

My constant and preferred companion on the hills during the last twelve years was, unquestionably, Josie, my dearly-loved partner and closest friend, who had never been up a mountain or fell before she met me. But, when she, sadly, died from a rare form of cancer in May, 2003, she had climbed many hundreds of them in Northern England and Scotland, enjoying every moment in the hills – except, now and again, when she was perhaps a little frightened by the exposure.

I was eighty when we met – twice widowed, irritable and crotchety, not as fit as I used to be, and convinced my mountain days would soon be over. But, entirely due to Josie, always happy and radiant with a lovely smile, I rediscovered my youth and returned to the hills with a new vigour. Through a lifetime of climbing and mountaineering I knew the hills intimately but now I was to have the wonderful experience of introducing my new partner – 14 years younger than myself – to their many joys, in all seasons of the year. It proved a rare delight – by far the best twelve years of my life.

Our first hill together was the spiky, little pyramid of Stickle Pike in Dunnerdale up which we dawdled easily on a sparkling, sunny day on 13 April 1, 1991 from Hoses farm. This had also been my very first hill nearly seventy years earlier – in a school party of short-trousered second formers led by our geography master, Mr H.M. Sawtell. I had chosen Stickle Pike as Josie's first hill because it had been mine and because of the long, interesting drive from my home in Kendal to Dunnerdale and the well-remembered delights of the Blacksmith's Arms in Broughton Mills to which we repaired on our way home.

It must have proved an interesting outing for Josie for, within the next few weeks, she was with me on Loughrigg (twice), Whitbarrow, The Calf in the Howgills, Wild Boar

Fell, the Coniston Fells, Black Combe and several others, usually going out at least twice a week. Josie had been visiting the Lakes from her home in Blackpool for many years for she and her husband, with their caravan at White Cross Bay as a base, had a yacht on Windermere and on many weekends she and her family were up in the Lakes, enjoying the countryside, especially the birdlife. But Josie had never been tempted to explore the fells.

Soon after these first outings together Josie was tackling the big hills with me – Great Gable, Helvellyn, Skiddaw, Scafell Pike and, sometimes, we were doing quite long rounds. Eventually I drew up a schedule of all the hills in Lakeland, the Yorkshire dales and the Northern Pennines more than 2,000 feet in height and we set about collecting them all. I had done them all – some of them many times – but it was a great joy showing them again to Josie. She was always enthusiastic but not very good at identifying hills – despite my constant and, no doubt, boring instruction on every summit. It didn't much matter to her what they were called. She just enjoyed being among them.

Fairly quickly we completed the ascent of the 40 peaks in Yorkshire over 2,000 feet in height and most of the Lakeland "two thousanders" of which there are almost 200 if you include every outlier. By 2002 she had done all of these except for a handful in the Pillar area, and the top of Scafell. On the day we went to collect the Pillar tops, walking from Wasdale Head, we decided to turn back on Looking Stead as we could hardly see through the sweat pouring into our eyes. It must have been about the hottest day that year and we were gasping for water. We told ourselves we would come back another day – but we never did. Scafell, too, being tackled from Eskdale, was abandoned on Slight Side, and we never managed to complete this one, either. I can't now remember our excuse for this failure for we were on ground very familiar to me with easy walking to the top. Perhaps we'd left things a little late that day.

I well remember Josie's ascent of Scafell Pike, again from Wasdale, for it took place on a really trying day – rain all the way up and thick mist on the top. This was the day following a sensational cloudburst over much of Lakeland and I have rarely seen the fells so drenched, with all the becks flooded, and many new ones sliding down the contours. Just before we set off from the car park near Brackenclose several Japanese walkers, all carrying umbrellas, walked past. They were followed by a very small Japanese person who seemed to be carrying all the rucksacks for the party. They set off up the track to Scafell Pike about five minutes before us but we never saw them again. What had befallen them I can't guess.

I remember we had quite a job crossing Lingmell Beck, getting wet through to the waist in a place where you can normally just stride or jump across. Perhaps the Japanese had been swept away. My photograph of Josie on the summit shows her happily waving something or other and her caption on the back reads: "Highest person in England – on top of Scafell Pike".

This was a red-letter day for Josie but her ascent of Ben Nevis, the highest mountain in Britain, turned out to be an even greater epic. We took seven and a half hours getting up and down the mountain and I told Josie, jokingly, that this would be about the slowest ascent and descent on record. But, reading a guidebook description recently, I noticed that seven and a half hours was given as about the usual time for the job, so we can't have done so badly.

Because she realised it was a great occasion Josie had put a Union Jack – a tea towel, actually – in her rucksack and announced she was going to drape it on the summit cairn. This she did and I photographed her standing proudly up there – the highest person, this time, in Britain.

As we were trotting down the mountain – there was quite a lot of snow on the upper reaches of the Ben that June day in 1994 – we encountered an elderly walker on his way down and chatted with him for a few moments. He then suddenly announced, with some pride: "Do you know. I believe I'm the oldest person to have climbed the Ben today". "Oh, yes", I countered. "How old are you?" And he replied: "Seventy one". He was quite non-plussed when I told him I could give him 12 years for I was then 83. I believe I was wearing my "Compo" hat which covers my bald head, at the time, and clearly had not looked my age.

Of course, all my hundreds of mountain expeditions with Josie were done when I was either in my eighties or nineties. But, perhaps, not very many in my nineties since we were, at first, bedevilled with foot and mouth restrictions. The hills, though, that we did climb together in my nineties included Ingleborough – Josie's favourite mountain, which, by then, she had ascended by six different routes.

After the Lakeland and Yorkshire "two-thousanders" we completed the 33 of them in the Northern Pennines and then did the Cheviot hills and quite a number of the Scottish Munros. We would have carried on with the Munros of which I had then done about 200 but after collecting a few of them in the Cairngorms we never managed to get back to Scotland for hill walking. And now, in my 94th year, I'm unlikely to go adventuring in the Scottish hills again – or perhaps any hills.

When we went into the hills together Josie would prepare a flask of soup or coffee and some sandwiches and put them in her rucksack. I'm ashamed to say that she nearly always carried the sack which also contained our waterproofs, "blow-up" seats for sitting on, bandages, hut key and several other essentials – including wire-cutters. These were, indeed, needed on one occasion when we were trying to negotiate a particularly awkward barbed-wire fence on Baugh Fell in Yorkshire.

Uphill, Josie went very well indeed but she was sometimes a little slow coming down and didn't like exposed edges or walking along the top of cliffs like the Wastwater Screes.

She was especially interested in birdlife, always noting the first cuckoo of the year and other bird sightings in her diary. I remember her excitement once on Naddle Fell above St John's-in-the-Vale when she found a skylark's nest, still warm, with an egg in it. And there was another day in Bannisdale when she spent much of a morning studying the soaring flight of a buzzard.

One day when we were coming down to Patterdale from St Sunday Crag I pointed out to her the little blue speck of Lanty's Tarn on the opposite side of the dale and told her the story of the tarn. She was so entranced by this – especially after we had visited the tarn a little later – that she decided to name a Kendal flat she had recently acquired, "Lanty's", and a friend carved a wooden name plate for her. But she never lived in the flat, having taken up residence in my spacious apartment soon after we first met, and she later disposed of "Lanty's" – a lovely name, I always thought, for a home.

Two or three times we lost each other in the hills – probably mainly because of my impatience. The worst occasion was when we went to visit The Howk, an interesting river walk near Calbeck where it was easy to go astray. As I was rather slow putting on my boots in the car park Josie said she would set off slowly so that I could catch up. I shouted something about waiting for me by the old mill but when I reached this she was nowhere to be seen. I suppose I panicked, thinking she must have tumbled off the rather steep track, and spent the next couple of hours frantically searching for her. Several times I went back to the start and then began asking local residents for help. Soon, half a dozen people were searching for her and when I was getting quite desperate and thinking of calling out the mountain rescue team, one of the Caldbeck villagers, who were all most kind and sympathetic, told me she had seen somebody who might be Josie walking down the track. So eventually, greatly to my relief, we found her. She had just gone walking on up the fellside and, when things got a little difficult, turned round and came down. Quite sensible, really.

There was another time when I lost her – again for a couple of hours – in the Whitbarrow woods. We were very familiar with this limestone hill, not far from our home, but not with the miles of woodland, threaded by narrow tracks, at the foot of the fell. Josie had left the path and gone into the woods, and, try as I might, I couldn't find her. I had tried to instil into her a drill for this sort of eventuality: "Always go back to the place where we were last together and wait there", but it didn't work this time. Nor did shouting and whistling. In the end, when it was beginning to get dark, and I was getting more and more desperate, we met, coming from opposite directions on one of the tracks. Again, she had shown much common sense when she realised she was lost. Coming to a junction of tracks she had made a cross of twigs to indicate the correct track and also marked an arrow on the ground. But it had been a worrying couple of hours. A third incident was on the slopes of Wild Boar Fell where we had been following parallel tracks a few hundred yards apart, for some reason. This time I was particularly worried because there were open pot-holes in the area but, again, it turned out alright in the end. Probably I'm an unnecessary worrier, but all three incidents seemed to put years on me. Josie was worried on each occasion but not nearly as badly as I was. She seemed to know everything would be alright – the difference, perhaps, between an optimist and a pessimist.

When we returned from these walks – after, perhaps a meal in a pub – we would read up the walk, or relevant parts of it, in one of the Wainwright books or one of my own, and I always wrote up the walk, very briefly, in my mountain diary. Later on I transferred all the walks with Josie – many hundreds of them – into a list, "Josie's Walks", on my word processor and this list I kept up to date. Our last outing together was the three miles round of Levens

Park, a few miles south of Kendal, at the end of October 2002 when we saw deer, goats, swans, kingfishers, squirrels and all the autumn glory of the colour in the trees.

So I only have to get out the yellow folder containing about 25 pages of these walks, with at least 20 walks on each page, to re-live, in the quiet of my drawing room, all those hundreds of walks with Josie, clearly recalling most of the incidents of those wonderful hill days.

THE MAGIC OF SNOW

Many years ago, when I was much more active than I am today, the most exciting moment of every early winter came when I first heard in the weather forecast on radio or on television the magic words: "Snow on high ground". Now, at long last, we could get down to what we enjoyed most – skiing or snow and ice climbing. I think you could say we lived for the winter: I know I did. And when, perhaps the next day, I saw from our windows the first snow of the winter, completely changing the familiar fells, highlighting the dark crags and making the hills look twice as big and twice as exciting, I was in my own little heaven. So, too, were most, if not all, of my mountain friends.

Snow, in those wonderful days, was an annual delight in the Lake District, that lasted up to four months in the year. I am not exaggerating. Thirty or forty years ago we used to count on up to four months of some sort of skiing every winter. You might have to carry your skis and the rest of your paraphernalia up perhaps 2,000 feet to find a small patch of snow on which you could just manage two or three turns. But, for us, this was enough to justify all the effort. And, sometimes, on the very best days, the skiing on, for example, Raise, where we had our tow, was almost as good as Glencoe or the Cairngorms or even Austria –although, of course, not nearly so much of it.

How things have changed. Last winter there were something like half a dozen or so days of skiing on Raise. The previous winter, perhaps a dozen days. And two skiing centres in Scotland had to close down through lack of snow. The pundits blame global warming and there seems to be nothing we can do about it. How long my club, the Lake District Ski Club – I have, regrettably, been extremely inactive for many years – will be able to continue to maintain their ski tow, to which so many years of effort have been devoted, is anybody's guess. Members now have to go to the Alps or further afield for their skiing.

I am trying to knock this out on my laptop – and think about snow – on a hot, humid June day with the windows open and a fan whirring away at my side. Not my sort of weather at all but millions adore it and spend all their money on expensive holidays to lie, frying slowly, on beaches. We, on the other hand, used to survive the oppressive heat and the sight of barely-clothed people in the street by looking forward to October with fresher weather and, hopefully, fewer holiday visitors.

PART FIVE

A Lakeland Year –
The Guardian, Country Diary pieces
1951 to 1979

JANUARY

1951

The friendly, sure-footed hounds of the mountain packs are not the only hounds out on the Lakeland fells these short winter days. Any weekend now you will see their first cousins, the faster, slimmer trail hounds, below the snow line practising for the coming season.

A slow job, demanding much patience, this training of a trail hound. When the puppy is seven or eight-months-old and has begun to hunt 'scents' in the lanes around the farm it is time to try it across a couple of fields, following the trail of an old stocking dipped in aniseed and paraffin. At first the little fellow is more interested in the piece of meat which he has seen the trailer take out of his pocket, but in time, after months of patient work, he will follow the trail for its own sake. Perhaps it is only a game now, but when he is an 'old dog' he will be ready to chase the sharp scent for 10 miles across the most mountainous country in England, without stopping to drink even on the hottest day.

And while the puppies are frisking about near the farm their elders, fat and sleepy after months of idleness and good food, are getting their weight down in practice trails higher up the fells. And there are two more months of this before the season starts.

1954

Before the heavy rains and driving snow blotted out the hills we snatched a short winter's day on the tops. At noon we passed an old man repairing a stretch of drystone wall, but we did not see another soul until we drove down the lane in the evening. The lights of the car picked out the lost remnants of a hunt in the shape of a farmer's lad with a couple of weary looking hounds at heel, on their way to a warm supper. The only other living things we saw all day were the sheep cropping the frozen mountain herbs and a pair of ravens wheeling above the head of the valley.

The pools in the winding track over the pass were iced over, and there were fingers of snow every few yards. Convoys of laden packhorses used to zigzag through these fells, but the only imprints we saw were an occasional half-moon of climbers' nails. It was biting cold on top and the wind, sweeping from the gaunt fells to the northeast, nearly took one's breath away.

The snow on the summit ridge was as hard as rock, heavily scored by the wind, and embellished here and there with little spillikins of ice which broke off under our feet and went tinkling down the frozen slopes in a delightful diminuendo of fairy music.

It was a relief to swing south at the farthest cairn, feel the wind at one's back for a change, and admire the view in comfort. The Pennines were hidden in a storm brewing up over there, but far to the south the flat top of Ingleborough was unmistakable, while a dozen miles away the old grey town squatted under a blanket of mist and fog with only the castle ruins peeping up above the gloom.

1957

From the valleys it appears that all the snow has disappeared from the fells, but it is still up there in patches if you know where to look. There was not a sign of it all the zigzag way up the pass the other blustery day but just over the summit we found a little, frozen drift pointing like a finger towards the north.

My border terrier reached it first and performed his usual tricks – scampering back and forwards, digging furiously, and rolling about in the snow on his back. Higher up the north face of the mountain I kicked steps for the fun of it across several snow slopes but the terrier preferred to take his own line. He would advance a few yards across the slope and then start rubbing the side of his body in the snow, just for the cold thrill of it. This invariably meant slipping out of his tiny steps and swooping down, out of control, on his back. He thought it was great fun, but after a dozen slides I got tired of fielding him from crashing onto the screes and chose a less interesting route up the outcrops and tussocks.

I saw the footprints of a fox in the snow and a skein of wild geese flew over towards the Solway, but the only wildlife on the fell was the fell ponies grazing down by the tarn. The terrier kept well clear of these. He remembers once trying to chase two of them, but they turned on him and gave him the fright of his life.

1963

The ice was rippled and pockmarked on one of our favourite skating places, but beyond the rushes on a roadside lake a few miles away it was smooth and black. Our blades sang as they cut the ice and the crisp air reddened our cheeks, but the principal glory was of the western sky aflame with an incredible sunset behind the purple outline of the fells, and later, of a glorious full moon shining down on the silvered ice and a stilled countryside. There have never been more perfect winter days in the fell country recently – days so beautiful that the wireless news seems to have been of another world.

Sometimes the east winds have been bitter and the snow clouds menacing, but, sandwiched between them have been still, sunlit days with skies of poster blue and distant snow-capped hills which seem suddenly to have leaped into the foreground.

From my windows I can see to the northeast a long line of smoothly sculptured hills – we used to think they looked like sleeping elephants – which have been snowbound, top to toe, for weeks, and, to the northwest, a wild trough of a valley winding deep into craggy mountains. Today there are only two colours in the distant scene – dazzling white and shadowed blue – but in the foreground there is welcome warmth in the rich browns of stately, old trees and the weathered grey of sun-splashed farm buildings. Two men are hard at work sawing an old tree for winter logs, and the shrill whirr of the saw is the only sound in a quiet, frozen countryside.

1966

The Lake District has never looked more wonderful in winter than it did just before the turn of this year. Each morning for several days we awoke to magical dawns, the slanting sunlight melting the last thin mists hanging over the fields, and all day long the snows on the fells sparkled in the sun with not a cloud in the sky and hardly a breath of wind. Twice over the holiday we were out on skis in the hills, but mostly had the snows to ourselves, and we drove back each evening through a quiet, still land with only the stars and a crescent moon for company.

These are the days for really long views. I haven't been on top of Scafell recently but I'm fairly sure Ireland, and perhaps Snowdonia, will have been visible from the summit during December, for I've seen them both from this point on similarly clear days. This week, without field-glasses, I could see the snow covered cairn on top of Thornthwaite Crag from my house which must be 11 miles away. But then, all at once, the skies darkened and the snows came down again and for two days the hills were hidden.

I cannot remember so much snow falling in the district before the end of the year. Each fall has been followed by massive thaws, and heavy rain, but the snow still lies deep in the mountains and this could be the longest winter in the hills for years. The December skating was, however, short-lived – just a couple of days after Christmas, and then the smooth black ice was quickly changed to treacherous slush.

But the outdoor man cannot grumble about the opportunities in the fell country this back-end, for he may well never see anything finer.

FEBRUARY

1952

Trudging quietly in the new snow, up through the woods to the skiing slopes, I edged around a shoulder of fell and suddenly found myself staring hard at a fine red deer only a few yards away. Before I could put down my load and reach for my camera he had time to give me a hard, disdainful look and threw up his head, silhouetted against the snow, in 'Monarch of the Glen' defiance. Then, dainty heels in a flurry of snow, he had disappeared.

Unless you go deliberately searching for red deer in their homes in the lonely upland corries of Martindale and Bannerdale or the Helvellyn woods you rarely stumble upon them on the fells. They are very shy, and unless the wind is in your favour they will know of your approach from more than a mile away. The snow had sent this fellow – with probably others of his herd – on a food-foraging expedition.

Contrary to one recently expressed opinion the red deer are by no means disappearing from Lakeland, and they are certainly widening their territories. They have crossed Ullswater to the Helvellyn mountains, wandered far south into the Furness home of the roe deer, and even reached the central Cumberland range.

But as much as we like the red deer the sheep farmer and the forester do not, so there is an excellent case for the establishment of Lakeland's first animal reserve. And what better place than Martindale, home of the red deer since medieval days?

1955

This wild weather must be terribly trying for dumb creatures. Today we came upon a lorry load of cows stuck in an 8 foot drift miles from anywhere in the middle of a bitter northeast wind. They had been up on that bleak moorland for two days and two nights, and every so often a cow-man had to squeeze into the box, milk his charges, and later give them their milk to drink. There was no other food.

Yesterday we found perhaps a dozen sheep huddled in the lee side of a fell wall, but slowly being covered by the blown snow. They preferred being blanketed with snow in comparative shelter to foraging beneath the shallower snow in the freezing wind. The mass of closely wedged fleeces did not stir but we knew they were all alive. In an hour or so they would be completely covered over, but the prospect did not occasion panic. They awaited their fate unblinking, glad for the moment of the warmth from the others. We told the farmer about them on the way down, but both he and I have known of sheep being buried for a fortnight and still alive.

On the frozen road a rabbit had been crushed by a motor car and already the crows, as hungry as all other wild creatures in the new white wilderness, were at work on it. The foxes will be coming down to the farms to look for poultry, for there must be little wildlife about, while the hounds are mostly in kennels these wintry days.

1956

The pine marten, they say, is around and about again on the fells. Some years ago he was thought to be extinct, but recently one has heard tales of huntsmen seeing a flurry of brown scurrying along an old stone wall, or the flash of his whitish chest as he wriggles down a hole. You don't go out to look for pine marten in the Lake District, but rather consider yourself lucky if you catch a glimpse of something that may be him. He must be the shyest of animals and there may be only a few handfuls of them hanging on to a precarious existence – probably in the comparative safety of the forestry plantations.

If hounds run one into a bield they seem to make even more fuss than if they had holed a fox. Perhaps the smell annoys them. This is understandable for the pine marten is only called 'sweet mart' because he is not quite so objectionable as his cousin, the polecat.

Sixty or seventy years ago pine martens were fairly common among the higher fells. I have not heard of the polecat being seen, but then he was more a creature of the marshlands and peat bogs. Many years ago they would be common enough, along with the wild cat, but those days, and the still earlier ones of the wild boar, are long passed. Strange, therefore, that the badger, once extinct, should be with us again, and now the pine marten.

1966

Although the casual traveller through the hills might not have always noticed the snow there has not been such a good skiing winter in the Lake District for years. Every weekend, starting with the first week in November, there has been skiing of a sort in the fells and there seems no reason why it should not continue for some time yet. Skiing in May is by no means unknown in the Lake District and it could happen again this year. It should not be assumed, however, that the skiing has been much like that pictured on the winter sports posters although there have been a few clear, sunny days when, apart from the absence of chair-lifts and the happy paraphernalia of Continental skiing, it has not been greatly different.

But there have been many other days of biting winds, thick mists, snow like polished concrete or just thin, soggy streaks of it winding through the boulders. Sometimes you have to climb almost to the top of the fells to find your patch, while on other days it has been difficult even to reach the snow since most of it has been blown into the roads. Occasionally, one has been able to get hauled up a practice slope on a length of thin wire or slippery rope but, for the most part, every yard descended has had to be climbed again with some labour.

There are no mountain top restaurants where flagging energies might be revived – a flask of coffee drunk standing up in the snow is the best luxury that can be contrived – and the après-ski is missing, but it's all very good fun for the young at heart who this winter have ranged from about three years to over seventy.

1968

Travellers from the south – which, to a Lakelander, means south of Lancaster – must have enjoyed one of the sights of a lifetime last Sunday if their journey took them over Kirkstone Pass or one of the other hill roads in the district. It was a foggy morning, demanding sidelights even along Westmorland byways and visitors had little hope of seeing even nearby fields and woods, let alone the high fells. But to a student of Lake District weather there could be hidden promise in the day, for not only was there not even a whisper of wind, but there was also the feeling that the fog could hardly continue up to the ceiling of the sky and that somewhere, high up, it might be a good day.

I drove through the gloom, with visibility down to a few yards, along winding lanes edged with patches of hard snow and then, halfway up the pass, came the miracle.

The first sign came over the tall larches that flank the pass – a tiny triangle of blue sky – and a second or two later I was driving through the top of the fog and into a new world. Slowly the grey curtain dipped down to reveal the sunlit snows of the Troutbeck fells, magnified through the framework of mist to look ten times their height, and above them the unbroken blue of the sky. The transition from Manchester gloom to a boundless Alpine panorama of white and blue and dazzling sunlight must have happened in 100 yards or so – a transformation the motorist rarely sees.

An hour later I was treading the highest snows in perfect weather, but the really exciting moment had been one which must also have uplifted the heart of many a city-weary motorist.

MARCH

1951

The young lambs are skipping about in the fields down by the river, but up in the fells and the remoter dales it is still too soon for lambing time. Even so, this next fortnight will be an anxious time for the fell-farmer, for more bad weather could mean heavy losses. The wind has swung away from the north, but the snow is still lying deep on the fells and we might get another fall any day. Already this winter there have been forty-nine falls of snow in at least one Westmorland village, and the shepherds say they have not seen so much snow for years.

Skiers have been enjoying the best Lake District winter they can remember, and in the north-facing gullies climbers have been out each weekend hacking steps up the steep ice-pitches and burrowing through the great overhanging cornices of snow into the winter sunshine at the top.

But hidden under the frozen snow many a mountain ewe, missed when the sheep were brought down to the lower fields, will now be lying dead, while others, far away from visible food, may be starving. One big Westmorland sheep farmer who in a good year can expect a 'crop' of 2,000 lambs refuses to forecast his chances this spring. There seemed promise in yesterday's warm sunshine, but today's biting rain spells more snow 'on the tops'.

1952

Up near the top of the pass the mist, swirling in grey, boiling clouds over the crumbling stone walls, was so thick that although it had been sunny five minutes earlier down in the valley I had to switch on my sidelights. A moment later I nearly ran into a man leading a trail hound, and then, a few yards from the summit, straggling along the side of the winding wall, there were perhaps a score of men in caps and breeches, each with his hound on a short lead.

Our hound-trailing season has not yet begun, but this was a practice trail and the 'trailer' with his odorous bag was due in from his long tramp over the fells in a few minutes. While we watched the men got their hounds into line, took off their leads, and waited, one knee on the damp ground, for the start. Long before the trailer appeared like a Brocken Spectre out of the mist you could tell from the excitement of the hounds that he was approaching. Then, suddenly, there he was, rather farther to the left than we had expected.

There was a sharp whistle in place of the dropped handkerchief and, with a chorus of delighted yelps, the hounds were away, leaping in a mad jumble of muzzles and legs into the whirling whiteness. There was nothing to see, so the men sat down to wait. But soon the hounds would be back, hearts thumping and coats soaked with sweat after their 5 or 6 miles run over the roughest ground in England.

1962

The daffodils are fighting their way up through the snow drifts at the bottom of my garden, and the forsythia and gooseberry bushes are budding nicely, but these are the only signs of spring in a still wintry world. All the main roads have been cleared of snow, but you can still get stuck in drifts on some of the minor roads and on several of the lanes leading to the remoter farms. A waterfall by the side of the pass not far from here has quite disappeared – first frozen over and then buried in a hanging drift – and all the becks are stilled.

I passed some sheep today, perhaps fifty of them, just brought down from the tops and feeding ravenously on piles of baled hay, but the birds, apart from the ravens, seemed to have been blown out of the sky.

Apart from the wind, whistling distantly through the crags, the countryside was strangely quiet and still – waiting, some dales folk will tell you, for worse blizzards to come. But the mountains are not so plastered with snow as one might have expected. Fierce northeasters have blown it off the fells and into the roads and the flatter intake fields so that, in places, it is easier to trudge up through the bracken and the heather than along the tarmac. The northern and eastern slopes are merely dusted with snow over the old drifts, but you can be up to your waist on slopes facing the sun within 10 yards of the car.

The sky looks savage tonight – a fiery orange flecked with angry black and grey. The winter is far from over.

1966

The most comprehensive study ever made of the hills of the Lake District has recently been completed by Mr A. Wainwright, of Kendal, after thirteen years of walking, writing, sketching, and photography. In nice time for the Easter invasion he has produced the last of seven little volumes which embrace the whole of the uplands between the sea and the Eden and cover more than 200 mountains. But the remarkable thing about these handy books that slip so conveniently into rucksack or pocket is that every page of them – something like 2,000 all told – has been meticulously printed or sketched by hand and then engraved by the block-maker. Not one word of type has crept into any of them, and the whole long job has been slowly done on a thousand evenings with pen and Indian ink. Mr Wainwright has spent most weekends at his desk putting it down on paper.

Thickly scattered through the books are hundreds of painstakingly drawn pictures of the fells, panoramas, routes, and most accurate maps, and no detail on a mountainside, waterfalls, caves, crags, quarries, tracks, and becks has escaped his eye. Even every wall, and every sheepfold, is shown. The only possible criticism of Mr Wainwright is that perhaps he has taken the adventure out of fell walking, but you can always leave his books behind and study them afterwards at your leisure.

1976

Nothing to be seen in Deepdale the other day except the swollen beck and sodden lower slopes reaching up into the thick cloud blanket. We squelched and felt our way below unseen crags into Sleet Cove and found the snow we had been seeking – a white, untrodden highway rising steeply between black rock walls towards a grey void. Would the snow gully reach the Fairfield Ridge without undue difficulties? We couldn't be sure for we were uncertain to a few hundred yards of our exact position but the snow, after loose scree and wet boulders, was a welcome change.

Crampons biting nicely into the hard snow we mounted steadily, pausing now and again to secure each other on the steeper sections. Every 50 feet or so we could see a little farther ahead through the gloom but the white ribbon continued unbroken. So much snow seemed unbelievable after all the rain and the knowledge that the south-facing slopes were completely bare. On we climbed, the cloud getting thicker until we could see only a few feet ahead, and then, after a final steep section where handholds had to be made, the gully flattened out and we found ourselves on an icy ridge.

I never cease to marvel about the extraordinary difference between north and south-facing slopes in our Lakeland winters. We must have ascended nearly 1,000 feet on unbroken snow on a day when motorists might have doubted the existence of a pocket handkerchief of the stuff. A quick compass bearing in an icy wind for the summit of Fairfield and we crimped across level ice to a familiar cairn and a decision on the best way down out of the clouds.

APRIL

1951

Although this has been another week of long hours of sunshine, and the cherry blossom across the road from my study is already making a brave show, there is still no sign of the famed damson blossom of the Lyth Valley. This is the blossom which every spring attracts hundreds of visitors to this quiet, softly wooded Westmorland valley, but the visitors have not yet been seen and the blossom is coyly awaiting even better weather.

"Top and bottom of it is t'wind's in t'wrang quarter," said the weather-beaten man in the big orchard near The Row. "Now, if it'd swing roond out o' th'east mappen we'd git blossom by next weekend. We allus reckon on aboot April 18 but this has been sic a terrible, lang winter with nobbut snaw, mizzle, and the like ivvery day it's a wunner t'crops are shapin' at a'."

With luck, the blossom should appear this year – as last year – without the leaf. If the leaf comes with the blossom – or before it as it did after the fierce 1946-7 winter – the blossom is partly hidden and does not make quite such a magnificent picture.

The winter continues to be quite remarkable. Only a few days ago it was still possible to ski from the summit of England for several miles along the tops, and it seems possible that patches of snow might remain in north-facing gullies as late as June.

1952

The short, black, long-maned fell ponies of the Lake District have started to foal again and the herd which, a few years ago, seemed likely to die out should be noticeably much larger soon. But I do not suppose there are any more than a hundred or so in Westmorland besides the herd of Shetland ponies which grazes high up on the slopes of Bowfell. There are perhaps about forty of these and I would not like to say which is the tougher of the two breeds. The little Shetlands seem to be completely impervious to the roughest weather and you will find them happily cropping short, sweet grass, their shining coats streaming with water and rivulets flowing down their noses on the wildest of days. When the snow lies in great drifts on the fells they may be brought down to the valley for feed, but normally they stick to their favourite grazing ground 2,300 feet up near Three Tarns. Here on better days they can munch the tasty turf in the late evening warmth until the sun dips down behind the wall of Scafell.

But the native fell pony – he probably originated from over the Border – can do a hard day's work on the farm, carry a 16-stone rider and never put a foot wrong on soft, loose or treacherous ground. I have even seen them ploughing. The remainder lead a gentleman's life high up in the Mardale fells or grazing zigzag up the lower slopes towards the summit of Helvellyn.

1962

From my window the last, faded remnants of a long winter are two or three tiny patches of snow hanging just beneath the plateau of the High Street range, and the daffodils are sprouting in the garden. Yet only five days ago we were floundering, not very far from here, in a foot of newly fallen snow and spring seemed very far away. It has been an odd winter – more snow than we have had for some years and some of the worst gales in memory, but the fell farmers have not been badly hit and some of the towns hardly affected.

Craftily, I have managed to get in some sort of skiing every weekend so far this year but this should not conjure up visions of sunlit snow slopes beneath bright blue skies. On at least half the occasions conditions have been unpleasantly Arctic with atrocious winds, although last weekend, for a change, we had deep, slushy snow and torrential rain. Even the worst days, however, have had their happier moments and I have many recent memories of the sudden lifting of heavy storm clouds to disclose brown, snow-flecked valleys smiling in the sunshine, or of distant winter views across half the Lake District and into Scotland.

Today, and for the past two or three days, the April scene has been traditional enough – wintry sunshine on the still brown fields, cloud shadows moving slowly across the fells, and peaceful mirrored waters.

And now the vanguard of the Easter invasion has reached us; rucksack-laden young folk hoping for fresh air on the heights, dry sunny rocks, hard ice in the gullies or – most optimistic of all – long slopes of crisp, old snow. I hope they are not disappointed.

1967

The best time for looking at waterfalls is, rather obviously, after prolonged rain or when the snows are melting. For it is then that such places as Lodore or Sourmilk Gill which, in dry weather, become disappointing trickles, are really worth seeing, while Aira Force or Dungeon Gill can nearly take your breath away. But none of these – and not even Scale Force, the biggest waterfall in the Lake District – can compare in seething power and crashing tumult, on the right day, with High Force, which carries the Tees down from the Northern Pennines along the Yorkshire-Durham boundary. The other day I drove over the Westmorland fells and down into Teesdale and took the opportunity to wander down through the woods to look at the Force. And it was well worth the threepence you pay at the entrance.

On most days High Force consists of one fall of about 70 feet on the Yorkshire side of the river and a trickle down the rocks on the Durham bank. If you are lucky, you might, in time of spate, see twin falls crashing down on either side of the crinkled precipice of basalt and limestone that juts between. But the other day the torrent was roaring over the whole width of the gorge, engulfing the crag in its headlong leap and thundering down into the river below with a roar that seemed to shake the ravine.

You can't see anything like this in the Lake District, and even the big falls in Scotland don't seem to have the sheer power and fury of this surging maelstrom when the flood waters of the Tees, fed by days of rain and tons of melted snow, fight their way through this narrow rock gap before their plunge into the depths. As you stand there, with the roar in your ears, the spray in your face and the brown, boiling fury only a stone's throw away, you wonder how many thousand gallons are going over every minute, and where you have ever seen such leaping fury before. "The finest waterfall in the kingdom", I've heard High Force described, and the other day this seemed no exaggeration.

1976

The holiday crowds had gone but there was a gentle trickle of walkers along the airy rooftree of Crinkle Crags and on to Bowfell on a glorious mid-week day of unbroken blue skies with views across several counties. Over the burnished sea we could see the Isle of Man and, across the Solway Firth, the dim shape of the Scottish lowland hills.

On the pointed peak of Bowfell – from many angles the most distinctive summit in Lakeland – a National Park warden, with splendid Alsatian in attendance, was collecting litter in a huge plastic bag. "Not so bad up here this holiday," he confided, "but Helvellyn was appalling the other day. Sacks of the stuff."

We discussed the shortcomings of some outdoor folk, the eroded condition of the tourist track up The Band, the growing nuisance of transistor sets on mountain summits. I told him that the rocks behind the Chock-stone on the so-called 'Bad Step' on the Crinkles had collapsed and there was now a new 'through' route for those too timid to tackle the little 10 foot wall. But footgear and equipment used on the tops this Easter, he said, had generally been good. The message, he thought, was at last getting through to the jeans and wellingtons brigade.

Snow patches still clung to the upper rocks of the Scafells and I could just pick out the last of the snow on Blencathra's Sharp Edge, 13 miles to the northeast.

MAY

1952

Darting and diving about our heads in bewildering trajectories yet miraculously never colliding, the swifts were enjoying their evening meal of the tiny flies carried up to the top of the crags by the up-rush of air in the gullies. Across the face of the crag, 300 or 400 feet below us, an old raven, looking for food, flopped along in his curious, awkward flight and then – conscious perhaps that we were watching – did a half backward somersault just for the fun of it. A perfect evening, with the far side of the tarn still catching the evening sun, so we hurried down for our first shivering dip of the season.

Refreshed and lazily smoking, the fisherman grumbled that he was carrying climbing rope instead of rod and line, for all over the tarn the trout were rising nicely, with tiny 'plops' and quickly widening circles every second.

We saw no char – those succulent Lake District fish – but we knew they were there, hiding in the shadows by the dozen. You may tempt them with the fly from the boulders on the edge, but down on Coniston Water or Windermere you go 'trolling' for them – a pleasant, lazy pastime for a peaceful summer evening.

How did the char get into this wild upland tarn? Some say the monks of distant Furness Abbey carried them up there long centuries ago.

1957

Today has been children's day at the great music festival in our little country town. From early morning youngsters from the villages and the dales, with new frocks and hair ribbons, well-scrubbed faces, and the light of battle in their eyes, have been converging on sunlit streets, en fete with flags and bunting, to make music, together and in competition. For some the day started with the dawn, but it finished for all with 600 country lads and lasses packed tight on a great concert platform and singing as they have never sung before.

There are a dozen simple little memories to last us until the next festival two years hence. The little boy with the merry brown face and red tie, for instance, singing with such assurance and skill that he later had to leave his lollypop and be dragged back onto the stage for a special word of praise. And the little girls, looking like angels, who sang a silly little song so sweetly – while watching their conductor as if their lives depended on it – that strong men could hardly trust themselves to speak. Then there was a school choir, whose members may be rascals at home, but who today had become so transformed that the judge, almost speechless, could find no word of criticism, and the little boys with their violins and cellos, who produced some peculiar noises, but so obviously enjoyed every moment of it all.

There cannot be much wrong with children who really enjoy making music, with the voices, with piano or violin, or even by blowing down a recorder – not while they are doing it, anyway.

1958

Sandwiched between the downpours of the last few days have been glorious hours when the Lake District has achieved an almost magical beauty. There have been times when all the well-worn clichés – skies of poster blue, clouds like cotton wool, and lakes like mirrors – have really come true. It is the rain which has brought out the magic

Sometimes after a soaking day the sunshine has melted away the dark clouds and revealed a smiling countryside washed sweet and fresh, with bright colours in the leaves and blossom, rivers in foaming spate, silvery glints on rain-washed crags, and new pools among the rocks. And, because there has been further rain on the way, the hills have stood out proud and clear with perfect, long-distance views into Scotland or out to sea.

One afternoon we peeped through the still glistening trees into a rain-washed dale flooded with sunlight. With their backs to the sun the fells reared up like purple giants while the grazing sheep, each ringed with golden light, took on a stereoscopic quality as if cut out of cardboard and placed in the foreground.

A red squirrel munching a coconut on a bird table shot us a mischievous glance and slithered in a flash into the cool, dark woods.

1964

You approach the site by driving or walking up steep fellside roads and the tree cover is so thick that you are almost among the chalets and the caravans before you notice them. To reach the campsite you have to climb still higher, and you find the tents snuggled down in little grassy hollows and obviously quite invisible from any roads or even footpaths. This, they say, is the best thing of its kind ever achieved by any National Park Authority in this country – secluded holiday accommodation to suit many types of open-air enthusiast.

On the day of the official opening I found one of the young campers, not at all interested in the speeches and a little disconcerted at the sea of umbrellas 100 feet below, cooking chips over a stove sheltered by a battered biscuit tin. From his tent flap he could look over Langdale Pikes, and a tumbled wonderland of low fells and woods, threaded by leaping becks, lay just below. Not a house or a road or even a telegraph pole in sight.

"I used to climb," he confided, "but I hurt my leg and we're sailing this time, on Windermere. They turfed us out of one field and told us to come here. I've always said I would not be seen dead on an organised site, but this is alright. You cannot even see the other tents...Yes, the view is fantastic, and have you seen the copper beeches further down the fellside, and the silver birches just coming out?... No, we do not mind the rain – we are used to it. If it keeps on I might buy a fishing rod."

And he turned his chips over in the boiling fat, carefully, one by one, with his knife, and then made room on the pan for two new eggs.

1977

Five summits in the Blencathra area, collected on a short May day of sunshine and storm, were the start of the modest but blatant peak-bagging challenge. The aim is to traverse all the 203 listed tops of more than 2,000 feet in the district within six months – a suitably pointless but conceivably enjoyable task for an old-age pensioner. All the ground has long been familiar but seeking new ways up and linking summits together in horseshoe rounds might require a little ingenuity.

An unconventional ascent of Blencathra by ravine and crag with a final scramble up the patchy snow still hanging like a tattered collar below the summit, was an encouraging start with close-up views of sheep clinging to the rocky upper slopes like the seabirds on St Bees Head. Not a breath of wind on top, dazzling sunshine on the snow patches, and unrestricted views for 30 miles but, five minutes later, a great black pall crept over the mountains and I was in a thunderstorm of driving rain and hail. Ahead, visibility shortened to yards but, curiously, through a bright gap below the black cloud to the south I could see the sun still shining on the High Street snow gullies. But the rigours of my new game meant a trudge across featureless moors to collect undistinguished tops around the desolate valley of Bannerdale before winding back along the skirts of the mountain wall to Threlkeld.

Few people nowadays go into these lonely dales in the corner of the National Park, but, 100 years ago, Bowscale Tarn, with its legend of two undying fish, was a big tourist attraction for Victorians.

JUNE

1962

It is a long time since the fells were so dry. Once merry becks are now stilled, waterfalls have dwindled to a trickle, and the foresters are worrying about the fire risk to their growing conifers. Six years ago, at a time like this, a carelessly flung cigarette-end started a fire which destroyed 140,000 trees in one Lake District valley, and thoughtless picnickers this weekend could easily wreak similar damage.

Critics of afforestation in the dales would have been pleasurably surprised had they been with me on a recent walk through one of our newest forests. The trees grow thickly around three sides of a shapely fell but there is no drab mass of unnatural colour, no regimentation of marching conifers, and no ugly skylines. Instead, I found the trees following the natural boundaries of crag, scree, bracken, and bog, with clumps of hardwoods or brightly contrasted single trees breaking up the spruce, and many gaps and ragged rides cleverly contributing to the planned disorder.

The rich greens of the beeches and the warm colourings of oak, birch, and rowan contrasted effectively with the spruce, larch, and pine, and an occasional Norway maple brought a splash of yellow sunlight onto the fellside.

Above the crowded woodlands the gorse fringed crags reared upwards towards a tumbled skyline, while at their foot the river narrowed into a rock girt pool where trout glide lazily in the shadows. This is the retreat for a Lake District heat wave.

1963

The wind, tearing in from the east, was so fierce on the crag that we had to balance carefully on our holds during the gusts and then climb upwards, as quickly as we dared, before the next gale swept upon us. The problem lay in deciding when and where to stop – here, on this awkward ledge, or can I reach that shelf 6 feet away before another gust comes along? To be caught by the worst of the wind when balancing upwards on toe scrapes seemed too exciting for comfort, and the tug of the rope, billowing out like a lasso, didn't help. We'd have been wiser to have looked at a gully climb instead – out of the sun, perhaps, but also out of this scouring wind. A tiny stone, dislodged perhaps by some walker on the summit ridge, whistled past our ears like a bomb. Things were getting unpleasant.

An hour later, battered and exhausted, we reached the ridge to meet the real wind – twice as strong as the gusts on the face, so that it was hard work merely to walk along the level. An angry personal wind it seemed – singling out each of us in turn and trying to wrestle him to the ground. A handful of birds were hurled haphazard across the sky, but nothing else seemed to be sharing our battle.

The Scafells looked calm and peaceful in the evening sun and huge white clouds rolled slowly towards the west. And far below the glistening black waters of the tarn looked strangely smooth.

We coiled the rope and fought our way, leaning on the wind, down the familiar slopes to the sheltered dale. The larks were singing across the moor and the insects buzzing in the heather. "Nice calm evening," they said down in the village, but we didn't want to argue.

1964

Lives have been thrown away for the edelweiss that grows on dangerous cliffs in the Alps, beckoning, white and silvery in its haughty solitude. Recently I bought two nice clumps of it in the market-place here for my rock garden. They are much better specimens of the plant than the little faded sprigs you are offered in the tourist shops in the Valais or the Stubaital. More than once, newly back from the Alps, I used to sigh for another sight of the gorgeous spring or summer flowers that always enrich the walk down through the moraines to the hut, but nowadays many of us have them in our own rock gardens. The rich drops of blue that are the gentians, spiking through the turf, the saxifrages, the primulas, the anemones, and the bluebells and a score of others. And even the most exotic of them can be bought at the nurseries, a few miles farther up the road from here into the hills.

In scores of visits to Scotland I don't think I've ever come upon white heather – really white heather – growing in the hills, but you can buy any amount of it in Westmorland. Indeed, it is grown here by the cart load for the Scottish tourist industry. But, so far as I know, nobody has started to cash in on the plant life of the Lake District to any great extent – Wordsworth's daffodils, the spring splendour of the gorse, the brave show of the damson in bloom, and the autumn glory of the bracken. We have our mint cake and our rum butter circulating pretty freely, but little else.

But I had forgotten. You can now buy tins of 'Genuine Lakeland Country Air' in many of our inns, but it was a London firm that thought up the idea. They're selling like hot cakes.

1972

When the moon is full and before the days begin to shorten that extraordinary Wasdale sheep farmer, Joss Naylor, intends to try to run up and down no fewer than sixty-five Lake District mountains within twenty-four hours. Last year, on a long day of low cloud, heavy rain and high winds, he managed sixty-one, defeating the long-standing record by only a short margin. But he is far from satisfied with this achievement. A strong walker might well be pleased with this bag of peaks collected in a month's holiday, but Joss thinks that, given good weather, he ought to be able to do better.

Joss, who suffers from cramp and a knee joint that keeps coming out when he runs downhill, lives for fell running, but has to fit it in while he is looking after 1,000 sheep, seventy cows and other assorted livestock – completely on his own. Several times, after winning some big mountain races many miles from home, he has had to hurry off before the prize-giving to get back to his milking. Once he was kicked on the leg by one of his cows so that he could only finish second instead of first as had confidently been predicted.

Joss is unlikely to run out of mountains on his latest attempt – there are seventy-eight tops in the Lake District of more than 2,500 feet – but one feels that he must shortly be approaching the limit of his endurance.

1973

The easiest way up Great Gable is to walk from the top of Honister Pass to the shoulder above Beck Head and then zigzag easily to the summit cairn. You can then traverse the mountain and return northwards over Brandreth and Grey Knotts to your starting point, making an easy circular, or elliptical, route among the fascinating scenery. It might be cheating to start from your car at over 1,000 feet above sea level but the elderly or infirm, if determined enough to walk the hill, have every right to cheat.

The outward leg takes you along Moses' Trod, a pleasant track that sidles around the contours and might, at one time, have been an old sledgate, a smugglers route, or a convenient way for plumbago pilferers or, indeed, and most likely, all three. Moses is a legendary character who might have made his whisky from the bogwater at the back of Fleetwith Pike, and the plumbago (or, locally, wadd) would have been stolen from the old mines at the head of Borrowdale in the days when a sledge-load of the stuff would have been worth a fortune. Clearly the track has been graded in places for ponies or sledges but, strangely enough, is not quite continuous and could have been in greater use 200 years ago than it is today.

The arguments still continue about whether Moses' business was slates, whisky, or wadd, or all three, but a strange imponderable is a 'Smuggler's Hut' perched among the upper rocks of Gable Crag. You could plainly see the ruins when I was a boy but little evidence is left today. Whether Moses or any of his predecessors ever used this remote eyrie and for what purpose is pure conjecture, but this still remains the highest building site in England.

JULY

1951

No dog works harder when called upon or is more deliciously lazy in front of the kitchen fire when off duty than the Lakeland sheepdog, and it seems odd that the same shaggy, honest-looking animal can also be glamorous. Perhaps the Lakeland dog which counts just now is the trail hound, while throughout the winter it is undoubtedly the foxhound of the mountain packs, but for a brief season, starting any time now, it is the turn of the humble sheepdog to catch the limelight.

Watch him at the trials in Rydal Park, on Applethwaite Common, or in any one of a dozen other beautiful settings and you will see him holding crowds of perhaps several thousand people completely spellbound by his intelligence and grace. You can almost hear an acorn fall as you watch him hypnotising a handful of sheep with one bright eye while with the rest of his personality he lures a single wayward Swaledale back to the pen. The flick of an ear or the quiver of a nose at the wrong moment would ruin everything. This is the moment when the shepherd, immobile beside the open gate, prefers to leave everything to Mick, Jup or Spot. The dog knows the job to be done and even seems to sense the vital ticking second of the watch in the timekeeper's hand. Speed is essential, but in these tense moments one must hasten slowly.

1953

The natural rock gardens of the high fells are perhaps at their best just now. Clinging to precipitous slopes between the outcrops there are fragrant clumps of heather in many colours (including white), patches of bilberry splashed here and there with the ink blobs of ripe fruit, tangles of bracken, perhaps a new sprout of mountain ash, damp beds of brightly coloured moss, a sprig or two of fairy fern, and tiny, shy mountain flowers peeping out among the rocks. The sight of such a corner in bright sunlight after a shower, with the dull colours of the washed rock richly glowing and a miniature waterfall glinting and dancing through the glistening foliage, is more rewarding than a view of some prize rock garden. No better heather grows in Scotland, but perhaps the Scots boast about theirs a little more.

It was just above one of these natural rock gardens that I found the other day what appeared to be the only sheep left on the central Lake District fells. All afternoon the shepherds, with their dogs skirmishing in the bracken, had been bringing down the sheep for the clipping, but this one had been missed. And instead of the summer music of 'baa' from every direction there was just this one piteous bleating from an old ewe who had mysteriously lost her lamb and all her friends.

Sheep-clipping is not quite the occasion it used to be when, after a gargantuan meal, the jollification went on all night, but there are still old men about who can sing, for instance, the *Martindale Sheep-Shearing Song*, composed by some unknown dalesman in the simpler days of long ago.

1955

It must be many years since we have had such warm weather for so long. Everywhere we see brown faces and, in the harvest fields and along the roads, the brown, glistening muscular backs of the workmen. We cannot remember a better hay harvest and already scores of fields give promise of a second crop. A drive along one of the valleys rewards you with the rich, sweet smell of new-mown hay, and in a motor-boat in the middle of Ullswater the other evening the same lovely summer smell came across the water.

On the shore shirt-sleeved holidaymakers mingled with the calm activity of the record-breakers or sat on the pier waiting for the steamer, but in mid-lake there was no hint of the excitements of speed or of the shrill voices of the crowds. Just a smooth, blue vastness stretching ahead, a duck on the water a hundred yards away looking like a twig, the steep winding path among the bracken on the hillside, smoke rising from the turrets where a twelfth century lord had his stronghold, and on the skyline the purple ramparts of the western fells.

The duck takes off in fright as we approach, its wings and feet thudding on the water as it gains momentum, and then sweeps in a long arc 2 feet off the ripples and swishes to rest again at a safe distance.

The sun glares down out of an unbroken sky; the only sound is the homely chug of the tiny motor and the only slightly foreign note a distant speck of yellow which we know to be a marker buoy for the speed attempt. Nearer the pier the brown-skinned youngsters, looking like Port Said ruffians diving for pennies, splash away without a care in the world.

1976

One way of tackling the hills during the recent heat wave was to get them in before breakfast. Moonlight ascents of, say, Helvellyn to watch the sunrise became rather commonplace, although Striding Edge at midnight could still be uncomfortably close and sticky. Swirl How by way of Wet Side Edge proved an easy night expedition, the only hazard being the sheep lying asleep on Wrynose Pass – generally in the middle of the steepest sections of the road. Why do these sheep prefer to sleep on tarmacadam or concrete in hot weather instead of in the soft grass? Can it be cooler? Rarely did the headlights or the engine noise disturb them, and as often as not, they would only consent to move when gently nudged by the bumper. Sometimes we had to stop to push them out of the way before we could get through the sleeping flocks.

Our dawn on this occasion was disappointing – nothing like so dramatic as one seen from Helvellyn, with the eastern sky gradually glowing a rich orange and then the sun suddenly peeping over the Northern Pennines. It is the change from the cold lunar light, with the hills in black silhouette and the moon shining on distant waters, to the blazing new sun flooding the valleys in warm, friendly colour that is so impressive.

Notable also on your return home in the bright, early hours are the shadows across the sunlight coming from strange, new directions, giving familiar views a completely different setting. This and the feeling as you come home for an early breakfast that you have somehow stolen an extra day.

1977

Heat surged out of the rocks as if from an oven, the fells shimmered in a blurred purple haze and there was not enough breeze to blow out a match. Not, perhaps, the best day for going around the Mosedale Horseshoe but in my childish pursuit, within three months, of the 203 'two-thousanders' it had to be fitted in.

Water, or the lack of it, was the problem. From the tiny summit of Steeple I peered down into corries that bite into the rocky north face of the Pillar range, saw glistening pools 1,000 feet below and listened, sadly, to the sound of distant falling waters. Too far off route to digress, I regretfully decided and later, from the summit of Red Pike, came to the same conclusion about the distant, beguiling waters of Scoat Tarn. The last and only water had been found near Black Sail Pass – this was an anti-clockwise round to keep the sun off my neck – and thereafter, one had to be satisfied with the mere sight of lakes and tarns miles away.

Everything seemed drier and stonier than usual, the rock ledges dusty, the bogs parched and cracked. On Yewbarrow I found a slimy muddy pool. Dying of thirst in the desert I might have drunk it dry; this time I merely dipped my wrists in the mud.

AUGUST

1951

Every summer day the young people, off to explore the Lake District hills, call at the little cobbler's shop in the centre of the village to have a few studs put in their town shoes or their brand new boots. Half of them have only the haziest idea of the pleasantest way up Helvellyn or Scafell – or, in fact, of any way – but they never think of asking the little old, spectacled cobbler with the gnarled fingers and torn apron. And, since he is not addressed, Ben (but that is not his real name), being a sturdy dalesman, would never dream of chatting just for the sake of it. But, it so happens, Ben knows more about mountains – and mountain wildlife – than most other men and certainly more than any of his customers. He is an authority in his own way on mountain birds and the geology of the district and he is a poet as well.

Very few dalesmen love mountains for their own sake as much as Ben, now nearing seventy. More than twenty years ago he climbed every 'top' in Lakeland, followed that with all the '2,000 footers' of England, and is now rapidly collecting the 500-odd 3,000 feet high points in Scotland – mostly in winter.

But the climbers whisper, "He's probably never been out of the village all his life" – and Ben is quite content to let them.

1952

A sunlit arena of close-cropped turf ringed by the fells where the bracken is just turning into its glorious autumn gold seems the perfect setting for the wrestling which has been part of the life of this countryside for centuries. From where we lie or crouch on the warm grass – the judges' view must not be obstructed – the wrestlers, gravely circling in their white tights and velvet trunks, or now and again pirouetting in a sudden whirl of arms and legs, blend into a frieze of athletes of ancient Greece until some shirt-sleeved, flannel-trousered dalesman spoils the illusion.

Undoubtedly there is more to this game than meets the eye. Watch an 18-stone giant apparently squeezing the life out of an opponent 4 or 5-stones lighter and there seems only one possible result, until with a deft twist the lighter man catches the giant off balance and they crash to the ground with the big man underneath. A shrug of the shoulders, a quick handshake, and the giant strides away, surprisingly nimble on his black-stockinged feet, while the winner collects his ticket for the next round.

Nothing is predictable, and a grey-haired dalesman of fifty who has merely removed his jacket and boots may well be a better man than a brawny, costumed youngster with sunburned shoulder muscles and bursting calves only half his age. Here, surely, is the cleanest sport in the dales and certainly the oldest.

1976

The fells swam in the heat haze, the towers of Calder Hall intruded dimly on the edge of the sea, and a transistor set incongruously intoned our Test Match misfortunes from the highest point in England. Down on Mickledore an inexperienced party could be seen and heard making heavy weather of Broad Stand, the easiest climb on Scafell, while halfway up the main crag two helmeted climbers were tackling the overhanging Flake Crack on what used to be the hardest climb in the country. The two were the only climbers on the face and from a sunny patch of turf on Hollow Stones, we watched them, our necks straining upwards, until they reached the traverses, with the finish in sight. They were testing courage and skill in a shadowed, vertical world; we were idling in the evening sunshine debating the contrasting attractions of a dip in Lingmell Gill and a long drink in a low-raftered inn. Finally we reached a compromise; we would do both – and we did.

Earlier, water had been the trouble, with the higher becks dried up but, underneath Pike's Crag, we had found the only spring – a half-inch spout of delicious ice cold water that made crushed sandwiches almost palatable.

The evening sunshine gilded the length of Wastwater, lighted the crags on Great Gable and, as we left, just tipped the topmost cliffs of Scafell.

1977

This weekend, with a day on Pillar Rock, I completed my self-imposed task of revisiting, within three months, all the 203 mountain summits in the Lake District that are more than 2,000 feet high. One of the last rounds was the collection of nine lonely summits in the 'Back o' Skiddaw' country – an area quite unlike any other part of the district and a blank on the map to most mountain folk. Here is a wild, untracked countryside of heather-draped fells, long deserted mines and unusually distant views.

As expected, I saw nobody all day – even in the distance – and nothing moved except the clouds and the quietly grazing sheep. From some of the heights – Great Sca Fell was one – I looked across the chequered Cumberland plains and the Solway Firth to the Scottish hills and, turning around, could pick out Bowfell and Crinkle Crags, nearly 20 miles to the south. There is a spaciousness about these views – mostly sky, flattened moorlands and vast stretching plains – that, except for the distant sea, reminds one of the broad acres of Yorkshire.

My day of high winds, sudden showers and scurrying clouds demanded careful compass work but the absence of tracks, cairns and litter was welcome after the over-used fells of central Lakeland. Even the sheep standing their ground or trotting up for a close inspection seemed unaccustomed to, or perhaps anxious for, human company.

Nobody seen all day, in the height of the season.

1977

Possibly the least-visited mountain summit in the Lake District lies, incongruously, within half a mile of the highest and most popular summit in England – Scafell Pike. Unnamed on the one-inch map but labelled Pen on the two-and-a-half-inch it is a fine, rocky summit perched high above Little Narrowcove – 'La'al Arra' to Eskdale folk – and separated from the Pike by some of the steepest and roughest ground in the district. People go up the Pike every day – many hundreds of them some days in summer – but I would be surprised if more than a handful go on to Pen in a year, and probably only the peak baggers even know of its existence. Appropriately, no tracks point the way and although the 2,500 feet high summit is graced by a neat cairn there are no beer-can rings, orange peel or sandwich wrappings to indicate the previous presence of civilised man.

My first acquaintance with Pen, many years ago, was following a day's climbing on Esk Buttress, the splendid crag below the summit, when the top merely provided a convenient resting place after coping with problems of verticality. Recently, however, ticking off the 'two-thousanders' of the Lake District, I had to seek out the summit again – this time from the Broad Crag col on a day of mist and rain. From the summit I could just see through the cloud the tumbled wilderness of upper Eskdale and, looking around, the dark crags below the highest place in England.

SEPTEMBER

1951

Very soon now the few visitors still with us will be admiring the lovely red cloak thrown over the autumn fells by the dying acres of bracken, but the Westmorland farmer cannot appreciate the russet glory, for bracken is perhaps his greatest enemy. Fifty years ago – even twenty years ago – the Lake District looked quite different from how it does today, for during the years the deadly spikes of fern have been marching boldly up the fellsides and swarming through the dales with almost tropical luxuriance. Every acre of bracken means so much less grazing and so much more cover for foxes, rabbits, and other vermin. Its only real use is to provide bedding for cattle, and I am convinced there is more than enough of the stuff in two or three valleys to bed down for the winter every beast in Argentina.

The trouble about the onward march of the invader –new acres are covered each year – is that there is very little you can do about it. Scientists have been trying for years to seek a reasonably economic method of clearing bracken, but with little success. Selective weedkillers have been tried and there has been talk of spraying from the air, but probably the best method is still the laborious cutting or 'bruising' two or three times a year for three years. And when the rough grazing includes two or three mountainsides the task becomes completely impossible.

1953

Although the golden eagle was finally driven out of the Lake District about 150 years ago, a holiday visitor now claims to have seen one only the other day at the head of the lonely pass which climbs over the fells from Grasmere to Patterdale. Well, this is not an impossibility but it is extremely unlikely. Almost certainly the visitor – who curiously, reports that he was using a telescope – saw a buzzard, which in flight almost exactly resembles the larger bird, and buzzards appear to be plentiful enough in the fells this year. On several occasions I have seen eagles in Skye and I have friends who know of eyries in Perthshire. They tell me there are strong reports of an eagle as far south as Ayrshire, and no doubt such a bird could easily fly to the Lake District, but the experts do not think he would. After all, eagles were reported in Wasdale two or three months ago and they all turned out to be buzzards.

200 years ago – according to Lake District parish registers – one received a shilling for killing an eagle, and the award for a fox was three shillings and fourpence. In spite of this encouragement to slaughter, foxes have continued to thrive, but the eagle, a creature of low fecundity, has gradually disappeared. Probably its end was hastened by the 'long, strong rope' kept in Borrowdale in 1785 for the purpose of 'letting down men into the rocks to take the nests and young of the eagles.'

1960

The agricultural show just up the valley takes place on a steeply-tilted field at the foot of the fells, for there's no level ground in the neighbourhood. When you drive in you take your car to the top of the slope for you know that if it rains – as it generally does – you'll never get out on the level, except at the end of a tractor rope. But by sliding downhill through the mire you might just manage it.

This is essentially a farmers' show – no stands or fancy marquees or sideshows or youngsters jumping ponies. Just the cows and then sheep and, almost apologetically, the sheepdogs. Oh, and a bit of wrestling this year, in case there might be some strangers uninterested in Shorthorns or Roughs. There's not even a notice on the main road to tell passers-by about all the excitement going on behind the wall, and unless you happened to hear the man with the loud-speaker calling, say, Class 22 into the judging ring, you'd drive right past the place. And only one tent on the field for president, secretary, judges, the press, or anybody else who wants to get out of the rain – that is, if you don't count the beer tent.

But to compensate there's a pleasant absence of restrictions – nobody to tell you where not to park your car and nobody even to keep you out of the judging ring, if you want to go there. Not to speak of the best show lunch in Westmorland.

Nobody is getting excited about it, but this is the centenary show. That's why the prizewinning cows and sheep are wearing coloured rosettes this year instead of bits of cardboard. But perhaps you didn't notice.

1962

One of the most useless pieces of weather lore to have by you so far as the Lake District is concerned is the couplet which begins; 'Red sky at night is the shepherd's delight...' As often as not the exact reverse is the truth, and this applies equally to the rest of the adage. There have been two good examples of the unreliability of this old saw within the last ten days – an incredibly shocking day following a magnificent golden sunset, and a bright, sunny day unexpectedly chasing an unusually vivid morning. All that one can do is to distrust a red sky most heartily whether it occurs in the evening or the morning, so that occasionally you might get a pleasant surprise.

'Too bright, too early', is often a fairly reasonable guide, while an exceptional sunset nearly always precedes a remarkable day. The unfortunate thing is that the day is just as likely to be remarkable for rain as for sunshine.

Farmers are popularly supposed to be infallible weather prophets but they must never be relied upon outside their own few acres. To them a patch of mist or cloud on a distant top or the wind coming from behind a particular wood might be of great significance, but take them into the next parish and they're lost. They might sniff the air, or throw straws into the wind, or even – although I've never seen them do it – put up a moistened finger, but they've really no more idea than you or me.

And you've only got to listen to the BBC forecasts to realise that the mountains make their own weather.

1976

You could describe Haystacks, sandwiched between the upper reaches of Buttermere and Ennerdale, as the biggest rock garden in the country. There is more heather on the fell than on many much bigger Scottish mountains, bilberries grow in considerable profusion, mountain flowers and grasses in great variety and even the main crags are unusually vegetatious. And, to complete the picture, the rocky outcrops that sprinkle the summit are linked by some of the most delightful pools in Lakeland.

A few hundred feet higher and Haystacks would be one of the great mountains of the district; as it is, many people would hardly call it a mountain, since it fails to achieve 2,000 feet. But it is certainly one of the best of the mini mountains – buttressed with great crags, crinkled with rocky lookouts, bespattered with tarns – including a perfect gem on the very summit – and surprises round every corner. Haystacks, in spite of its height – and partly because of it – is also one of the superb grandstands of the fell country. From its knobbly summit ridge are remarkable close up views of the dramatic sides of the big mountains – Scafell, Great Gable, Pillar and the Buttermere fells. And from where else can the climber see, in one glance, the cliffs of Scafell Crag, Gable Crag, Pillar Rock, and Boat Howe?

From a distance Haystacks, with its dark colourings and sunless crags, sometimes appears rather sombre but once on the fell, even in the worst weather, you discover warmth and intimacy.

OCTOBER

1958

My border collie is just over a year old and we have had him about a month. By breeding and in appearance he is a sheepdog but he was said to be disinclined for work and not really interested in sheep, which seemed to make him an ideal companion for the fells. It would be cruel, I think, to keep a dog purely as a pet when all he really lived for was working sheep. But although Sambo will never be a competitor at the sheepdog trials – unless he changes very quickly – he is nevertheless very much aware of sheep. Sometimes even a grey boulder in the distance will excite him and he will notice a Herdwick a quarter of a mile away, but twenty of them in a frightened group may not even cause him to lift his head. I have walked him, off the lead, through a whole flock of sheep without his appearing to notice them, but a lone sheep, scampering behind a rock, might stir his interest.

Small children are his heroes, bacon rind his favourite dish, and training to the whistle his delight. Already, within a month, I can bring him to me in the dark with one whistle and stop him in the distance with another. To me, previously more accustomed to terriers, his intelligence is uncanny. After a few lessons he was stopping at the edge of the kerb before crossing the road, and we think he now knows the meaning of perhaps a dozen English words. But we will never know what goes on inside that fine, alert, black and white head, nor what those bright, brown eyes have seen.

1963

The clocks go back tomorrow night, small boys have started hauling bonfire material along the lane, and the fell packs have begun another season, so that winter's not far away. The weekly newspapers now give their 'Hunting Appointments' with times and places for those who want to join a hunt – or watch from the car, as so many do nowadays. Every weekday from now on at least one fox – and possibly several – will be running for his life across the fells which is not a pretty thought, but then neither is the widespread slaughter of lambs and poultry.

One newspaper publishes a picture of an opening meet – the master, the huntsman, and the whip, well booted for the fray with sticks in one hand and glasses in the other, all ready to move off. With them are the hounds, sleek enough now and rid of their summer fat, and the little tousled terriers with their sharp, beady eyes peeping through fierce, tufted brows. This particular huntsman has been at the game for forty years and has perhaps accounted for as many mountain foxes as any man in history. A short, stocky man in heavy boots, baggy breeches, old coat, and red hunting cap with a haversack on his back and a short crop and lead in his hand. Very few people know more about terriers than this quiet-spoken dalesman who can tell you the characteristics of each one of his hounds. He will spot a fox streaking into a distant borran before you or I could focus our eyes and he knows these fells as well as some people know their back gardens. And until somebody can think of a better way to deal with foxes he and his kind will continue to perform a very useful service in these parts.

1970

Among the best places to visit on the right sort of day are the rocky coves scooped out of the east face of the Helvellyn range. While scores of people are walking the rather uninteresting summit ridge or scrambling along the well-trodden tracks over Striding and Swirral Edges the corries, largely trackless and, except for the tinkling of becks, quiet as a cathedral, can be quite deserted. You can see the walkers on the ridges, small as matches, but they probably can't see you, swallowed up in the wilderness of rock, bracken and grass, and the craggy fellsides shut you off from the bustle of the most popular mountain, even in high summer.

The best time is the morning, with the sunlight flooding the coves and highlighting the eastern crags, but the rewards can be enjoyed in any month of the year. A bright morning in early spring, with the longest lasting snows in the district reaching down into the corries and the ice glistening in the gullies, would be my favourite, but last weekend was a fair substitute. The waterfalls in Ruthwaite Beck were in noisy spate as we left the main track through the valley but the silence by Hard Tarn was only broken by the croak of the ravens as they tumbled across the sky.

Hard Tarn, an oval jewel caught on a rock ledge just below the topmost crags, is one of the least visited tarns in the district. The other day it reflected all the colours of the hills and the sky – an upland miniature of Lanty's Tarn down among the Scots pines near Grassthwaite Howe, which we passed a couple of hours later before returning to civilisation by the Grisedale Beck.

1976

Hounds were out on Whelter Crags above Mardale, the red deer had gone to ground, but the fell ponies grazed, undisturbed, high up in Riggindale. Mardale Waters, the cluster of teeming becks east of the High Street ridge foamed and leapt down the contours towards the largest reservoir in England, but the sheep grazed amongst the ruins of the farms flooded so long ago, and you could see the old lanes again and recall memories of the drowned dale. Haweswater, a mile shorter now than its length on the map and only one-third full will take a long time to recover.

I chose a sporting route up the craggy north face of Harter Fell – a rocky watercourse, a damp gully, an airy ridge and a bonus of clean, rough rock – and, from the summit, looked down on the now ugly bare, grey shores. On to Mardale and High Street and easily down Long Stile and Rough Crag to the valley.

The dalesmen, scanning the fells through fieldglasses for a sight of the hunt, had gone, but the car trippers were there –searching unavailingly, for eagles. High up at the head of Riggindale, with no hunters about, I had come across two of the hounds, frenziedly quartering the steep screes and baying as they went, but the fox eluded them. They would have a long, lonely walk back to the kennels – hours after the rest of the hunt.

Mardale with its ring of lonely fells maintains a largely unspoiled beauty and quiet serenity.

1978

There was far too much water crashing down Borrowdale's Sourmilk Gill the other day to make its ascent a reasonable expedition. But in drier weather this can be a feasible and enjoyable route for the competent climber-scrambler seeking an unorthodox way to the heights. Moreover if this semi-aquatic introduction can be combined with the ascent of Rabbit's Trod, a moderate climb up the northern flank of Gillercomb Buttress, the summit of Grey Knotts may be attained after 1,800 feet entirely on rock – an almost unique opportunity in the Lake District. By avoiding most of the gill, where a bathing costume would have been appropriate, and the upper pitches of the climb which were wet, it was nevertheless rewarding, on a warm, sunny day after heavy rain, to make at least half this height in scansorial fashion. Easy rock with its changing, little problems delightfully eases the ennui of endless grass or eroded tracks.

Two climbers met on top of the Buttress had travelled from Stirling for the weekend. "We got tired on Glencoe in the wet," they explained, "so we came to the Lakes where the crags are lower and drier."

From Brandreth the dome of Great Gable blocked the view to the south but elsewhere the giants of the fell country, Pillar, Great End, Skiddaw and Helvellyn, straddled the horizon, bathed in the afternoon sunlight. School parties, anxiously shepherded by their teachers, crept down the Green Gable ridge but Base Brown was deserted save for a worried couple, off route and trying to find Honister Pass. Down at the bustling Seathwaite road end the narrow lane was packed tight with cars. The first really fine day for a fortnight had brought out the worshippers in force.

· NOVEMBER

1954

Peep into many a Westmorland home nowadays and you will discover in the place where you might have expected the television set an awkward looking hand-loom and perhaps in another corner an object more quickly identified as a spinning wheel. Elsewhere such apparatus might have been imported to add a touch of warmth and realism to a room filled with old brass and willow-pattern china, but here they are meant to be used. More people in these parts than you might guess have taken to weaving their own wool.

One farmer's wife – there may be others – has made herself completely self-supporting so far as clothes are concerned. When she requires, for instance, a new winter skirt she collects the wool from her own Herdwicks, cards it, cleans it, spins it, dyes it with lichen, gorse, or bracken roots according to the colour desired, weaves it into cloth on her own hand-loom, and then makes the garment.

This revival in craftsmanship is not confined to the womenfolk, and I have talked to men proudly wearing suits they have made themselves from balls of wool. And in many cases they had made their own looms too.

It is said that the Westmorland archers at Flodden and

on many another field wore Kendal Green, and today, in farm and country houses, their descendants are making the same strong cloth and dyeing it with green weed to give it just the right shade.

1957

Snow has not yet reached the Lake District dales, but the first flakes have fallen on the fells and winter cannot be far away. A few days ago I was crunching over snowdrifts 3 feet deep on an eastern summit overlooking the Eden and trying to face into a biting northeast wind. The summit may be reached by car – if you are on official business – by means of the highest road in Britain, for a radar station is perched up there – 2,780 feet above sea level. Men are at work there, day and night throughout the year, providing navigational aid for unseen aircraft, and the low buildings are easily the highest continuously inhabited place in the country. The other day the 120 foot high latticed steel masts were hanging in ice and the station looked like a Siberian outpost, but down in the valley it was a pleasant, sunny autumn day.

On our way to the station we watched for a while aircraft which need neither navigational aid nor engines – the lovely, soaring planes of the local gliding club. Soundlessly they sailed over the edge of the fell from their launching point, swept gracefully across the gorge, turned, hovered and swooped, and finally crept silently in to land.

It was dusk by the time we were down from the high snows and, driving south across the moor, we watched a glorious sunset.

1962

Hopes of a Lake District skating carnival this weekend have been washed away by today's thaw but a few people were able to try out their blades before the rains came. And there is a skiing meet in the Helvellyn range on Sunday – the first in November for years. One wonders whether heavy snowfalls so early foreshadow a severe winter, but not even the farmers claim any reliable evidence and such doubtful signs as an abundance of berries may be largely discounted.

The snow caught most of us unawares and even the official warning from the meteorological people arrived too late for the taking of such precautions as the salting of the roads, highways were soon blocked – Kirkstone Pass for five days – and there were the usual infuriating hold-ups and delays on the main trunk road into Scotland. How much longer have we to wait before the Minister announces the line of the proposed motorway northwards through Westmorland, and a start date for the work of construction? The present delays due to the steepness and exposed nature of the Shap Fell route already cost many tens of thousands of pounds each winter.

But even the worst weather has its compensations, and the sight of the snowbound fells during the still days gladdened the hearts of many. For there is nothing in our Lake District scenery to compare with the glory of the sunlight shining on mountain snows with blue, cloudless skies above and sleeping, mirrored lakes below.

1974

The climbing of the highest mountain in the world by its most difficult route – 'the last great challenge left to man' – is being planned in a converted cottage at the back of Skiddaw. Here lives Chris Bonington, leader of next year's expedition to climb Everest by its formidable South West Face – five previous attempts have failed – and here he is working on the complicated details, immersed in paper and the irritants of telephone and typewriters.

Directly behind his remote cottage rise lonely fells, seldom traversed by tourists, and from the top he can look south to the Lakeland hills. Sometimes, when he wants to think out a problem – how many carries, for instance, from Camp 4 to 5? – he walks up the long grassy slopes, while at weekends, for harder exercise, he is climbing the Cumbrian crags with members of his team. One of the fifteen young climbers – the oldest, the ubiquitous Hamish MacInnes, is forty-four while the youngest is only twenty-three – could well be the first Britisher to stand on the summit of Everest, but this, says Bonington, is not the major aim.

"Our sole objective," he says, "is to climb the mountain by the South West Face because, at the moment, this is the most challenging unsolved problem in mountaineering. We are not climbing the mountain for nationalistic reasons but, if we get to the top, it won't do Britain any harm – especially just now."

John Peel, the Cumbrian the world knows best – because of the song – lived and died not far from Bonington's retreat, and they say that 3,000 people attended his funeral 120 years ago. Chris is not yet quite so famous but, at forty years of age, he is not doing so badly.

1976

Wonderfully rewarding to sit on the summit cairn of Brown Pike only a week ago, stripped to the waist and basking in the warm sunshine. Not a breath of wind, Blind Tarn, far below, a black mirror burnished by a segment of sunlight, and the crags of Scafell, blue-grey against the autumn gold, looking almost within throwing distance. Then, a couple of hours later, during a leisurely round of the Coniston fells standing in the crisp snow on the north side of Swirl How and looking across the whole of our mountain heritage from Skiddaw to Morecambe Bay.

There have been several recent days like this in the fell country – days of fog and morning mists in the valleys but cloudless blue skies, unbroken sunshine and lonely quietude on the tops as the hills settle down to their winter sleep. Strangely, the Isle of Man which, on a clear day, peeps over the summit of Grey Friar from this viewpoint, was invisible, hidden behind horizon haze, and the line of the temperature inversion hung across the sky suggested a weather change soon.

Too perfect on the sunlit tops to hurry down at dusk so we did the last hour in the dark, stumbling over a black shoulder of the fells.

DECEMBER

1955

Eight great sleek salmon lay like blackened logs in the shallow waters of the pool just below the waterfalls. In that small place, darkened by an overhanging mountain ash, they looked like young whales. If you threw in a stone they would glide lazily away, and perhaps one would break the surface as he turned, showing you his long, dark glistening back. They had come a long way from the sea to this lonely valley – something like 40 miles from the Solway Firth by way of the Eden, the Eamont, the Lowther, and then this straggling beck.

Each year some tremendous force which we can only guess at prompts these salmon, somewhere out in the Irish Sea, to risk this long journey in a distant mountain stream. Some people say they always come back to the river where they were born. Once they have started on their long journey there is no turning back. Waterfalls, weirs, and shallows have all to be tackled in their turn.

It was daylight when we saw the salmon, and they knew we were there. At night, however, it is different. You can wade into the pools, almost among them, and they will not stir – a fact of which the poachers are well aware. Sometimes they creep along the beck at night, shine a hooded torch into the likeliest looking pools, whip out a salmon on the end of a barbed gaff, and pop it into their sack.

1956

There was snow on the tops, ice-hard on the ridges, and long white fingers probing down the gullies recently, but soon after we had deluges, gales which rocked the house, snow, ice, humidity which made the bedroom walls stream, sunny Alpine mornings, and bleak, miserable dark afternoons. Earlier on huntsmen coming over the passes with a full pack of hounds lost nearly all in the storm, squelching down into the valley, battered and drenched, with only one couple and a terrier or two. The remainder have been popping up all over the Lake District since.

Another day, two lads camping out on the high fells in a schoolboy test spent a wretched night holding down a gale wrecked, sodden tent, after a crawl on hands and knees in a wind they had not believed could exist. But then the sun sparkled on the new snows, and after there was not a hint of wind, only the black ice on the pools.

This is the season of the hunt balls, the shepherds' meets, the village whist drives, with turkeys, geese, and chickens as prizes, and the ploughing competitions. 'The champion ploughman of the world' competes at a local village event which has been an annual affair for more than a hundred years.

1958

We left the fog which filled the whole valley, drove for ten minutes towards the north, and then, leaving the car, climbed up a grassy track zigzagging into the fells. Soon the fog was well below us, a dirty white blanket hiding the little towns and villages, and the fells, with their crazy walls, stood up all around us, smiling in the pale afternoon sunshine. Below us, too, we could see the high road over the pass, with tiny toy cars moving silently up and down.

A few small patches of snow lay, like pocket handkerchiefs, just below the highest summit, and the smoke from the farmhouses down in the valley rose straight upwards and then hung in the air like the armful of cloud just hiding the roof of England. Not a whisper of wind, and not a sound except now and again the spatter of the dog through the pools or a sheep rustling through the dry bracken.

Down in the lane we had passed oak and beech still wearing their withered leaves, ash, blackthorn, and hazel, but on the fell only an occasional bare, wind-blown larch, then a lone rowan by the side of a beck and then nothing but the bracken and heather. A pair of noisy ravens shattered the silence near the top of the fell and then, a wonderful sight – a flight of perhaps thirty geese in clumsy arrowhead formation honking southwards across the sky.

1975

Loughrigg Fell is the sort of place that determined mountain men are inclined to avoid – a low, sprawling upland, crisscrossed with paths that lead nowhere. But, on a short, misty afternoon at the end of the year humble little Loughrigg seemed to have a quiet serenity – even a touch of magic – not always found on the high fells. The several summits command extensive views of the mountains, but it is nearer scenes that provide the engagingly intimate quality of the fell – peeps down into less frequented corners of smaller lakes and tarns, into stately woodlands and even into the well-kept gardens of fine county houses.

There are probably more footpaths to the acre on Loughrigg than on any other fell but, so varied and personal are the vistas, that you almost have the feeling you are on private land. Every little rocky top reveals a new picture, a well-clipped hedge, a sloping lawn, a summerhouse or a shallow tarn in the middle distance, and you seem to be in a specially privileged place, halfway between the mountains and gracious country living. And this feeling seemed heightened this quiet December afternoon by the banks of low white cloud that hung above the valleys, making the high fells seem remote, in another world, and the skirts of the fell the boundary of this special place, so close to busy highways.

1976

Overnight the snow blanket on the fells had changed, as if by a magician's wand, from knee-deep powder to hard packed crust – perfect for winter mountaineering. From the icing sugar cairn on Dow Crag we looked north across miles of untracked snow and distant black cliffs to the roof of England and south, beyond soft brown valleys and dark misty woodlands, to the sea. Beneath our feet familiar gullies, packed with snow, plunged between icy walls to the black pool of Goat's Water and we assessed the pitches for a later ascent in this best outdoor winter for years. Looking down on Low Water later – frozen, this time, right across with white ice – we pondered on the difference in water temperature caused by an extra 200 feet in height.

A pair of ravens – they mate for life – followed us along the ridge, occasionally giving an aerobatics exhibition above the corries and, many thousands of feet higher, silent aircraft crept across the blue zenith like silver darts in slow motion.

As the sun sank behind the Dunnerdale fells we strapped on crampons for the descent of a steep gully of frozen snow on a shadowed east face. No sound except the satisfying crunch of pointed steel on the smooth white carpet and the hiss and slither of chips of ice sliding down towards the darkening valley. The descent taking longer than expected it was dark when we reached the intake fields. Coniston, not far below, looked a cluster of fairy lights and, over our left shoulders, the North Star high above Wetherlam gave us another bearing.

PART SIX

Coniston Tigers Log Book Notes
circa 1932

[Undated entry] G.A. and J.A. also started on a series of excellent 'tours de force' perhaps most remarkable of which was the ascent in boots under rather intimidating circumstances of North Gully. G.A. led, and when asked for his opinion of the climb, pronounced it, "Not too hard."

About this time too, Geo. Basterfield, G. S. Bower and Bentley Beetham, (who took part in the 1924 Everest expedition) renewed acquaintance with the crags. At first they were content with climbs of the calibre of the much travelled Woodhouse's 'B', but a week or so later, we espied them high up on Broadrick's 'B'.

A week after the ascent of Hopkinson's Crack by D.B. and G.L.J. (who incidentally came up in boots) A.H.G. attempted to lead up L.K.G. , below the 'Bandstand' however, the leader, found considerable difficulty with the pull-up on the right-hand 'pinch' hold and was forced to give up the attempt, swearing to come back later.

On the same day too, A.H.G. , doubtless inspired by J. H. Doughty's article on 'failures' in the FRCC *Journal*, made an abortive attempt on the severe variation of the second pitch of Woodhouse's 'B'. Doubtless, J.W.D., who was climbing second, could have led the thing easily enough, but with characteristic reserve, he preferred to leave the decision to the unworthy scribe. A.H.G. led J.W.D. up Southern Slabs using the 'George' belay.

At Whit. weekend, G.A. and J.A. made an expedition to the Napes, with the aid of pushbikes as far as Middlefell. The day was one of terrific heat, and the party, who were on their first visit to these crags did well to do the two West Chimneys – (K.K.W.W and Eagles Nest W.W.). They returned, vowing to renew acquaintance at an early date, with the Wasdale crags. Later G.A. and J.A. climbed Hopkinson's and Southern slabs on Doe, finding little difficulty with either.

J.W.D. now decided to keep away from the hut for a time until his exams were over, but kept in touch with the gang by seeing T.T. and J.W.P. and the Barrow crew at intervals.

Round about this time L.B. returned to form and led J.W.D. up Arête, Chimney and Crack.

At the hut everything was progressing on sound lines. Golf seemed to be the reigning passion, G.A. and D.B. proving sound exponents, while others, of the calibre of the scribe, merely lost the balls.

However, in one glorious swing, A.H.G., doubtless by a 'fluke', managed to hole out in one at the third 'hole', in a round with T.T. but, with his next shot, at the short fourth, he drove down a rabbit hole, and, as T.T. had already put one into a swamp, play finished. An alternative course was constructed by G.A., and weekly J.A. improved.

Bathes in the lake sometimes three times in a weekend were frequent, but L.B. and others were looked on askance when they actually appeared in bathing suits – of the Riviera type, too!

T.T. was often absent and, on occasions, tax collecting had to be undertaken by accredited substitutes. The purchase of fruit tarts from the farm, often added interest to Sunday night dinners!

The hut received a nice winter 'coat', and, at a later date the place was disinfected and the entrances improved by the laying of gravel 'drives'.

One of the beds broke down, but as the numbers seemed rather lower than during the spring, sleeping accommodation for all was generally available.

11 June

A.H.G. went to Wasdale for a week, renewed acquaintance with many good friends, and made some new ones. Most of the Napes climbs and the Nose (North) and West Wall on Pillar were led, and he was led up North West by G.S. Sansom.

With L.K.G. an attack was later made on this climb, but rain at the start necessitated a postponement – a very fortunate move as the party later ran into a cloud-burst on Looking Stead.

N.B. – North West is a wonderful climb – with exposure rarely met with on Doe. A.H.G. estimates it easier than Doe 'very severes' – mainly awkward and exposed cracks and chimneys.

'Nose' on the North is one of the finest movements the scribe has ever come across in climbing.

On the Napes, Rainbow, Cutlass, Scimitar, Sabre, Chantry – in addition to the more familiar climbs i.e. Eagles Nest etc. – can all be well recommended. A little loose rock on top of Rainbow and Sabre needs care.

N.N.B. (for fell walking enthusiasts): Lingmell climbed from Hotel – 1 hour 25 minutes, there and back.

L.K.G. does not recommend camping on the valley side of Ritson Force – mad cows and sheep!

18 June – was wet, and the party did not stir from the hut, except for a walk by two members to Coniston.

18 – 25 June

Wednesday. Foul day. J.W.D. and A.H.G. went up by 5.25 train and had to be satisfied with the ascent by variation start of Gordon and Craig in pouring rain. Later Great Gully was done, and J.W.D made an abortive attempt on the severe variation. Rocks slimy.

Later A.H.G. was struck when climbing up slabs at the right-hand gully exit, by a large stone – his narrowest escape.

On the way down the party rescued two crag fast sheep off 'A' Buttress.

Friday. A.H.G. led L.K.G. up Raven, Central, Central Chimney, Broadrick's 'B' and the party made the third ascent of Tiger Traverse.

N.B. Line should be used for Broadrick's 'B'. At the stance 40 feet above the keenly anticipatory second (Doe

Crag guide) the leader should reach high up in a vertical crack, on the left, facing the rock, where will be found a jammed stone. A line can just be jammed behind this, and the leader can sit and bring his second up what is perhaps the hardest pitch. This belay is not mentioned in the guide, but is advised.

25 June
G. Anderson, J. Atkinson. G.L. Jones, D. Birch, L. Brown, J.W. Diamond, A.H. Griffin.

A glorious day! G. Anderson made fourth recorded lead of Tiger Traverse and then led J.A. up Broadrick's Crack. Used left wall quite a lot and pronounced the climb, "overestimated".

A.H.G. got in his long cherished 'lead' of Hopkinson's followed by J.W.D. who could reach the vital hold in the severe pitch below the 'Bandstand' from the ledge. Before this the party climbed North Wall – a delightfully exposed climb, with a good 100 foot run-out for the leader, and followed by the descent of Black Chimney (J.W.D. last man). Later J.W.D. led Branch – his first severe lead.

In the meantime G.L.J. had made history by leading direct finish to Murray's. He went up the layback part in fine style but found considerable difficulty with the 'easier slabs'. The whole thing is certainly very severe and very exposed.

L.B. had a good day with George Bower doing the Hawks, and Murray's Route, but D.B. was off form this day, although he got in his, "usual Sunday afternoon walk."

2 July
G. Anderson, J. Atkinson, D. Birch, A.H. Griffin.

Once again we fell in with the three 'B's' – Basterfield, Bower, and Beetham – and once again G.A. showed that youth goes hand in hand with energy.

G.A. led Easter Gully direct, Trident and other climbs too numerous to mention – (I am losing count of some of his ascents). A.H.G. led D.B. up Murray's Crack, and later led a Preston friend up Murray's 'B' while D.B. took another one up Central Chimney.

At the hut, on the Saturday evening, members were intrigued by a weird cry coming from across the lake. Later it was found to have been a friend of A.H.G. 'yodelling' from nearly 3 miles away.

9 July

G. Anderson, J.Atkinson. D. Birch (from Sunday). T. Tyson (until Sunday) A.H. Griffin and L. Brown.

T. Tyson was persuaded to stay the night but left on Sunday morning. Most of the members had three bathes over the weekend, despite the rain which rather spoiled climbing on the crags. D. Birch arrived late on the crags from Barrow.

A meet of the F.R.C.C. – many people including the two 'B's' being on the crags.

G.A. led J.A. up Central Chimney in boots while A.H.G. and L.B. went along to North Gully. After getting as far as the cave, they could see that an ascent was unlikely as a miniature waterfall was coming over the severe slab.

D.B. then led A.H.G. and L.B. up Gordon and Craig, and after the find of a pocket signalling torch the party trooped down to the hut.

Hargreaves and party made attempt on a new climb to left of Trident, but were beaten by the wet rocks.

N.B. During the past few weeks little has been seen of J.W.P. but great things have been heard. Among other things, he has led Pinnacle Face direct to Hopkinson's Cairn and done some good work on Doe particularly on G.C.R. (Fuller reports unavailable).

PART SEVEN

**Selection of walk route notes from
Harry Griffin's walking diaries, 1977 to 1999**

The following walk route outlines are from Harry Griffin's personal walking diaries, brief notes that he assiduously wrote down in two thick notepads for more than twenty years and at times referred to for his writing. Selected from hundreds of entries these cover a wide range of Lakeland and might be of interest for readers to plan outings on the fells, after reference to appropriate guidebooks and Ordnance Survey maps as necessary. These are not detailed route notes, but give some indication of days that Harry enjoyed on the fells; on the honeypot summits such as Helvellyn, visiting hidden corners like Lanty's Tarn, and also exploring the Back o' Skiddaw country, where quiet and solitude can still be enjoyed and the absence of a multitude of cairns would meet with Harry's approval.

- 1977 May 10 – From Wrynose. Cold Pike, Red How, Great Knott, Pike o' Blisco.
- 1977 October 2 – Eagle Crag from Stonethwaite. On to Sergeant's Crag, High Raise. Down by Greenup Gill
- 1978 May 18 – Brown Pike, Dow Crag, Coniston Old Man.
- 1978 July 18 – From Haweswater. Nan Bield, Mardale Ill Bell, High Street, Rampsgill Head, High Raise, Kidsty Pike
- 1978 October 26 – Fleetwith Pike from Gatesgarth and Haystacks. Down by Scarth Gap.
- 1979 August 11 – Gasgale Gill, Hopegill Head and Whiteside.
- 1980 April 17 – Thirlmere to Harrop Tarn and Blea Tarn. To Ullscarf, Greenup Edge and back by Wyth Burn.
- 1980 August 10 – Little Town to Maiden Moor, High Spy, Dale Head and Hindscarth.
- 1980 September 3 – Blencathra from Scales via Sharp Edge. On to Blease Fell and down by Scales Fell.
- 1980 October 4 – Ullock Pike, Skiddaw, Bakestall, Whitewater Dash.

- 1980 October 11 – From Carrock Mine. Carrock Fell, High Pike, Knott, Great Calva.
- 1981 May 14 – Bowscale Fell from Bowscale, Bannerdale Crags and down east ridge.
- 1981 June 10 – Around Seathwaite Tarn from Wrynose Pass and ascents of Grey Friar and Great Carrs.
- 1981 August 29 – Watson's Dodd from Stanah, Great Dodd. Down by Stanah Gill.
- 1981 September 10 – Gray Crag from Hartsop, Thornthwaite Crag, High Street, Satura Crag, Brock Crags.
- 1981 October 9 – Whiteless Pike from Buttermere, and Grasmoor. Down by Lad Hows ridge.
- 1981 October 23 – From Honister. Brandreth, Grey Knotts, Green Gable, Great Gable, Beck Head.
- 1981 December 9 – Striding Edge, Helvellyn and Swirral Edge.
- 1982 April 24 – Robinson from Newlands and Dale Head.
- 1982 June 17 – From Braithwaite. Grisedale Pike, Eel Crag and Causey Pike.
- 1982 October 28 – Langdale Pikes via Jack's Rake, Rossett Pike, Hanging Knotts, Bowfell.
- 1983 January 18 – Loughrigg from Elterwater. Return over Silver How.
- 1983 January 29 – Steel Fell, Calf Crag, Gibson Knott, Helm Crag.
- 1983 July 28 – Pike o' Blisco from Wall End.
- 1984 August 4 – Great Dodd and Clough Head from High Row. Return down coach road.
- 1985 March 20 – Old Corpse Road from Haweswater to Swindale and Selside Pike.
- 1985 May 31 – Scafell Pike from Seathwaite. Up by Grains Gill. Down by Corridor Route, Styhead.
- 1986 August 8 – High Rigg to Tewet Tarn and back by St John's Vale.

- 1987 January 30 – Up Hart Crag (Woundale) from Kirkstone to Caudale Moor, Thornthwaite Crag, Threshthwaite Mouth and back.
- 1988 May 28 – Mellbreak from Loweswater and back along shore.
- 1990 August 5 – Black Combe from Whicham.
- 1991 June 19 – Wetherlam. Up Wetherlam Edge, down south ridge.
- 1991 August 30 – Place Fell from Patterdale to Sandwick and back by shore path.
- 1992 June 15 Robinson from Newlands. Down by Littledale Reservoir.
- 1993 October 13 – Whiteless Pike, Wandope and Crag Hill.
- 1994 January 10 - From Glenridding to Lanty's Tarn and back by Grisedale.
- 1994 January 16 – Wansfell Pike from Ambleside.
- 1994 July 23 Birkhouse Moor and Catstycam from Glenridding.
- 1994 August 21 – Skiddaw, Little Man, Sale How and Lonscale Fell from Gale Road.
- 1995 June 7 - Kirk Fell from Honister Pass. Ascent and descent via Beck Head.
- 1995 June 22 – Esk Pike via Grains Gill and Allen Crags
- 1997 June 15 – Fairfield by Tongue Gill and down by Stone Arthur.

INDEX